"An incredible and indispensable resource. Biegel and Cooper are exemplary guides using compassion and grace in supporting teens struggling with self-harm. Packed with highly relatable and accessible tools, teens will learn not only to be incredible survivors, but to perfect their 'awesome sauce recipes' as well! Teens, parents, therapists, and caregivers will equally benefit from the invaluable tools that integrate mindfulness and much more in this workbook."

—**Goali Saedi Bocci, PhD**, licensed clinical psychologist, and author of *The Social Media Workbook for Teens*

"Biegel and Cooper have captured every possible helpful angle to help teens who struggle with self-harming urges and behaviors. Loaded with personal self-harm assessments and a wide range of highly effective, easy-use strategies, this workbook leaves nothing out. I highly recommend it for teens, therapists, and educators seeking a workbook that delivers much needed coping strategies to those who self-harm and to those seeking to truly understand it."

—**Jeffrey Bernstein, PhD**, licensed psychologist, author of *The Stress Survival Guide for Teens, Mindfulness for Teen Worry, Letting Go of Anger for Teens Therapeutic Card Deck*, and *10 Days to a Less Defiant Child*

"With loving confidence Gina Biegel and Stacie Cooper guide teens through a step-by-step exploration of their worth in this practical and supportive book. Helping people overcome self-harm without inflicting additional blame and shame is no easy task, but in speaking directly to teens in language that is simultaneously clear and nuanced, direct and compassionate, the authors have managed to create a voice worth trusting, a sense of collaboration in the process, and an invitation to step into healing at one's own pace"

—**Jennifer Cohen Harper**, founder of Little Flower Yoga, author of *Little Flower Yoga for Kids*, and coauthor of *Yoga and Mindfulness Practices for Teens Card Deck*

T0299453

"*The Mindfulness Workbook for Teen Self-Harm* is a wonderful and practical guide, not only for teens/adolescents, but really anyone looking to better understand themselves and to effectively manage overwhelming feelings/stressors, constantly arising in today's fast-paced, stressed-out, modern world. The authors have taken a very difficult subject to talk about—self-harm—and have, with open hearts and arms, taken it out of the dark and shined a healing light on it. They have created a brilliant and creative step-by-step guide to help those struggling in darkness to find a way out of their pain and suffering, back into the light. It is written in a way where one feels as if the authors are right there with you, holding your hand, guiding you every step of the way without judgment, just love and support. Highly recommended for anyone wanting to help heal their emotional pain and suffering."

—**Alexander Bacher, PsyD**, clinical psychologist at Passages Treatment Center in Malibu, CA

"This book makes a perfect complementary resource for student support teams in middle schools and high schools, or for any other helping professional working with teens. Gina and Stacie's warmth and sincerity permeate the pages as they soothe and gently guide readers through activities to help them understand the relationship between stress, trauma, thoughts, emotions, and self-harm. Readers will learn how to nourish themselves using a variety of mindfulness strategies, including how to 'take in the good' for more well-being and peace."

—**Tracy Heilers**, executive director of Coalition of Schools Educating Mindfully

"As a researcher of social and emotional learning and mother of two teen girls, I literally breathed sighs of relief while reading this workbook. It opens up exactly the conversation that teens, parents, and professionals need to have about normalizing and facing with compassion the dark thoughts that teenagers have always had. Whereas we used to think that doing so meant approving and encouraging self-harming behaviors, we now know the opposite is true. Biegel and Cooper strike the perfect tone while providing gradual action steps that will unquestionably resonate with the teens of today, and bring relief from suffering that can feel insurmountable."

—**Amanda J. Moreno, PhD**, associate professor and founder/director of the Social and Emotional Learning Initiative at Erikson Institute

"Adolescents have needed Biegel and Cooper's *The Mindfulness Workbook for Teen Self-Harm* for years. The book is a masterpiece, with dozens of meaningful exercises and ways for teens to relate to what is going on inside of them. The clarity of the authors' writing and experience with teens shines through every page. Explaining thoughts, emotions, and judgments through activities will enable readers to embody what they learn. The ideas in this book will help young people stop and think before they engage in self-harm. Teenagers are hurting desperately, and the number of young people engaged in self-harm is alarming. This book should be on the shelf of every counselor and therapist. Parents and teachers should be trained in these practices so they can help their children and students build healthy self-images."

—**Laurie Grossman**, director of social justice and educational equity at Inner Explorer, Inc., and cofounder of Mindful Schools

"This workbook attends to the needs of teens who self-harm, with the embodied practice of mindfulness: compassion, non-judgement, and presence. Teens will feel supported and empowered as they are held in the wisdom of Gina Biegel and Stacie Cooper. Like breadcrumbs intentionally left to create a path, the authors use practical exercises and deep understanding to guide teens to their own inner knowing—a place where they can not only survive, but thrive. All preteens and teens could benefit from this thoughtful, inspiring, and healing work."

—**Lisa Grady**, chief strategy officer for Inner Explorer, Inc., a nonprofit changing the World, One Student at a Time Through Daily Mindfulness

"Gina and Stacie have written an incredibly important workbook offering very practical mindfulness strategies to help teens overcome the damage that comes from all manner of self-harming behaviors, thoughts, and feelings. This book will have a lasting positive empowering effect on all the teens, parents, and professionals who read it!"

—**Todd Corbin, CPC**, is a mindfulness teacher, motivational speaker, certified parenting coach, and author of *Mindfulness for Student Athletes*

the mindfulness workbook for teen self-harm

skills to help you overcome cutting & self-harming behaviors, thoughts & feelings

GINA M. BIEGEL, MA, LMFT
STACIE COOPER, PsyD

Instant Help Books
An Imprint of New Harbinger Publications, Inc.

Publisher's Note

This publication is designed to provide accurate and authoritative information in regard to the subject matter covered. It is sold with the understanding that the publisher is not engaged in rendering psychological, financial, legal, or other professional services. If expert assistance or counseling is needed, the services of a competent professional should be sought.

INSTANT HELP, the Clock Logo, and NEW HARBINGER are trademarks of New Harbinger Publications, Inc.

Distributed in Canada by Raincoast Books

Copyright © 2019 by Gina M. Biegel and Stacie Cooper
Instant Help Books
An imprint of New Harbinger Publications, Inc.
5674 Shattuck Avenue
Oakland, CA 94609
www.newharbinger.com

Cover design by Amy Shoup

Acquired by Jess O'Brien

Edited by Karen Schader

FSC
www.fsc.org
MIX
Paper from
responsible sources
FSC® C011935

Library of Congress Cataloging-in-Publication Data on file

Printed in the United States of America

24   23   22

10   9   8   7   6   5   4   3

To all those who have or continue to self-harm, there is a way out of the pain and shame. I take a deep bow to those who are seeking recovery from self-harm. There is a way out!

With admiration,

Gina

I dedicate this to each of you who had the courage and desire to pick up this workbook—to each of you who has the desire to make positive changes in your life and within yourself—you are a survivor and deserving of all the beauty life has to offer. You've got this!

With love and respect,

Stacie

contents

Section 1: Self-Harming Behaviors

Section 2: Be Mindful, Not Harmful

Section 3: Self-Harming Thoughts and Feelings

Section 4: Take Control of Your Life

a letter to teens

Congratulations on taking the first step to learning, growing, and changing. Even if this book was given to you and you don't know why, you are here right now: we encourage you to continue reading and see what happens. What you learn might challenge you and ask you to look at and handle things in new and different ways than you may have in the past. It is when you are open to learning new ideas and information, to becoming the author of your own story—a story of awareness, openness, trust, survival, healing, growth, and love—that you can begin to grow and change. We look forward to taking you on a journey of self-discovery, growth, and rising strong.

how to use this book

The best way to use this book is to work through the activities from start to finish, as each activity builds on the ones that precede it. If you come to an activity that doesn't fit, you can move on, but we encourage you try it first unless it triggers you to want to harm yourself in some way. Sometimes it might help to stop an activity, take a mindful pause or break, and then return to the activity.

This book is *not* meant to cause you additional pain or suffering, or be an opportunity for you to be hard on, shame, or blame yourself—quite the opposite. This book is meant to help guide you on your journey to be a survivor and rise strong. In many activities, you can begin to do things differently, and to stop, or at least reduce, your stress, pain, and suffering. This is you beginning the change process. Give yourself time, and be patient with yourself.

In each activity in this book, you will find a mindful takeaway in the moment: These are quick points that we consider important information or key takeaways for a given activity. The takeaway might include a sentence to help sink in a point, or it might ask you to do something in your day that can help make an activity more useful and valuable to you. You can refer to the resource pages in the back of this book for additional support and guidance. You can also use the extra journal pages in the back whenever you want. You'll find a host of additional materials for download on the website for this book at http://www.newharbinger.com/43676.

celebrate yourself

We know change can be hard. We applaud you for your bravery and your willingness to consider change and to see things differently. Be kind to yourself—and be patient with yourself. Real, lasting change doesn't happen overnight. Celebrate your efforts and your wins along the way, and be forgiving and compassionate with yourself if you have setbacks.

Warmly,

Gina and Stacie

PS: We too were your age once; we remember our own struggles with anxiety, worries, depression, sadness, feelings of being alone, and other such pains in our own younger years. Why do you think we are writing this book? We are guided in our work by this quote: "Be the person you needed when you were growing up."

to professionals, parents, and caregivers

We are grateful that you have chosen to use or share this book with a teen who is struggling. We hope this book will provide you with a myriad of tools to guide them through a mindful way to ending self-harming behaviors, thoughts, and feelings—they are usually all connected. Our intention is for teens to stop harming themselves and to get at the roots that led to these behaviors in the first place.

We seek for teens to first become mindfully aware of their self-harming behaviors and the choices and actions they have been making (Section 1 of this book), prior to actual behavior change. We next provide alternate tools—mindful practices, interventions, and related strategies—to eliminate and minimize these self-harming behaviors (Section 2). We then want teens to get at the underlying thoughts and feelings that often precede self-harming behaviors to ease their mental and emotional pain (Section 3). Finally, we encourage teens to take control of their lives, to help them survive and rise strong through self-harming behaviors, thoughts, and feelings with the use of positive strength-based practices (Section 4).

to clinicians, health care professionals, and helping professionals

There is flexibility in how you approach this workbook, especially depending on your profession and experience working with teens and the specific topics in this book—self-harm and mindfulness. You can start using the activities from beginning to end or do what feels right and use a specific activity that stands out to you or seems like the best fit for a teen. There are two caveats: First, if a teen is triggered in any way by an activity, we encourage you to table it for the time being. You can always return to it at another time. Second, the mindfulness-based activities in Section 2 do build upon one another. It is like strengthening a muscle—you would want to start with a lighter weight and build up to a heavier weight; similarly, you want to build the muscle of mindfulness.

to parents and caregivers

To parents and caregivers, thank you for seeking knowledge and guidance. If you have a teen or know of a teen who is suffering from self-harm, we strongly encourage you to seek the support and guidance of a mental health or related professional. Please refer to the resource pages in the back of this book as a preliminary guide to getting assistance. We always suggest erring on the side of caution! This book can assist, supplement, and complement mental health treatment, but it is *not* a stand-alone treatment tool or a replacement for treatment.

We are grateful, humbled, and honored to work alongside you throughout this journey.

Warmly,

Gina and Stacie

trauma and mental health treatment: what this book is and isn't

Trauma is the result of an overwhelming amount of stress that exceeds a person's ability to cope with, manage, or handle it. Each person responds to stress differently. For example, a particular stressful situation might be traumatic for one person and not for another, and reactions can vary: a racing heartbeat for one person and a downright panic attack for another. Trauma can be seen or unseen, inflicted by another person or people, or even self-inflicted—in the case of self-harm. Trauma can affect someone both physically and psychologically. The effects of trauma can be short-lived—acute—or long term and enduring—chronic. People differ in how they are affected by and respond to trauma.

Trauma can be roughly divided into two general categories: physical and psychological. *Physical trauma* is a serious injury to the body—for example, sexual or physical abuse, substance use or abuse, scarring, cutting, or burning. *Psychological trauma* is when one's mind is damaged, impaired, or affected because of a distressing event.

These two types of trauma sometimes overlap. Psychological trauma may be the result of a physical trauma or an injury to the body, or it may be the result of people, places, objects, or events that are unrelated to any physical injury; for example, it can be caused by another person's words or actions, as in emotional abuse or neglect. In these cases, emotional or mental trauma can be harder to detect because it might not physically hurt or leave marks (self-harm is one way of creating these marks). The psychological trauma someone experiences might be kept from their conscious awareness as a protective mechanism to keep their brain and body safe. If it is not in their awareness, people who experience psychological trauma may have a more challenging time recovering from it. This type of trauma may come back to revisit a person years later in nightmares or flashbacks.

trauma and self-harm

There is often a connection between trauma and self-harm. Not everyone who has experienced trauma will engage in self-harm; but often in one form or another, a person who has experienced or is experiencing trauma, without proper assistance and treatment, might turn to self-harming behavior to cope with or manage the effects or pain of the trauma. Someone may also engage in self-harming thoughts and feelings to try to manage the pain resulting from trauma.

The connection between trauma and self-harm must not be taken lightly. If you are engaging in self-harming behaviors, thoughts, or feelings, you may very well have some level of trauma in your past, or trauma that may still be taking place. In this case, please ask for help and seek mental health assistance. It is imperative!

seeking mental health assistance

This book can be used in two ways. First, it is *not* meant to take the place of mental health treatment, but it can supplement or complement mental health treatment with a helping professional. Working through some of these activities might bring up painful emotions or memories that require the support of a mental health professional. Please explore these issues with a mental health professional or an adult you trust, or refer to the resources section in the back of this book for phone numbers and websites to contact if needed. Second, this book can be used on your own, but you may want to seek out the support of a family member or adult you trust if your emotions become heightened or if you find that difficulties arise while you're reading or working through any of these activities.

take control of self-harm: be a survivor and rise strong

Mindfulness is about becoming more deeply aware of the moment as it is unfolding, to notice what is already present to be noticed—your senses, thoughts, feelings, and physical sensations. Mindful awareness is the first step toward change. This book is a guide to being a survivor—that is, continuing to function and do well despite past or present self-harming behaviors, thoughts, and feelings. The four sections in this book guide you through the steps to becoming a survivor.

Step 1: Have mindful awareness of your self-harming behaviors, thoughts, and feelings.

Step 2: Stop engaging in your self-harming behaviors, thoughts, and feelings to the best of your ability.

Step 3: Learn and engage in healthy ways to cope with and manage your pain and suffering without self-harm by choosing to do something different.

Step 4: Move through, overcome, and grow from the harmful experiences—rising strong.

how this book can help

This book can help readers identify, manage, and move through self-harming behaviors, thoughts, and feelings. It is not a treatment for trauma, nor is it going to resolve the effects of trauma. It may lessen the intensity of the effects of trauma, but those who are traumatized most often need the assistance of a mental health professional and the support and love of trusted others. If you are reading this and feel you have no way out, or are being or have been traumatized, please seek mental health assistance. Although we—Gina and Stacie, the authors of this book—aren't with you right now, we want you to know that even if you feel at your worst possible place, even if you feel self-loathing, shame, or like you are unlovable, we will love you and hold you in our hearts until you can love yourself—that is our promise to you!

pledging a pause to self-harm

To truly give these activities the opportunity to work and for you to fully benefit from the journey of learning, discovery, and change, we, the authors of this book, ask that you take a pledge to pause self-harm. If you are willing, we ask that you sign and date the appropriate lines below; you can also download a copy at http://www.newharbinger.com/43676.

If you have signed this pledge and do engage in self-harm, please do not beat yourself up; change takes time and courage. Your willingness to change, and your agreeing to pause self-harm, is what we are asking of you.

I, _____, pledge to pause my self-harming behaviors to the best of my ability.

Signed by _____ Date: _____

if you're not ready to sign this pledge

If you don't feel comfortable signing this pledge now, you can (1) come back to it when you do feel ready or (2) consider a *self-harm reduction plan*. Of course, it is our preference that you will pause self-harming behaviors and sign the pledge, but this readiness may come with time and trust in the materials you will be reading.

self-harm reduction plan

It may be too overwhelming to go from relying on an unhealthy behavior like cutting, drinking, or using drugs to quitting it cold turkey at the snap of your fingers. If you find it's too hard for you to completely stop right away or to be consistent, you can put yourself on a self-harm reduction plan. Start by taking baby steps. For example, if you have been cutting your arm, perhaps you start by replacing this with a less-harming behavior, like rubbing ice on your arm, holding ice in your hand until it melts, or putting a rubber band around your wrist and snapping it when you have the urge to cut.

Think about whatever this behavior might be for you. How can you work to do it less frequently, for less time, or in a less harmful way? Write your initial ideas here.

_____

_____

_____

_____

_____

What is it like for you to think about reducing your behaviors over time and giving yourself permission to slowly make positive changes?

_____

_____

_____

_____

Don't be too hard on yourself if you slip up or give up, thinking you are a failure or not strong enough. There is no shame in being human. If you "mess up," it doesn't mean you are a "messed-up" person. Every person on the planet makes mistakes. Everyone has moments where they do the thing they know is bad for them.

What matters is that you are aware of your actions and recognize that you have the power to make a different choice next time. The fact is that you are working toward doing self-harming things less and less often and replacing them with healthier behaviors that help you flourish and thrive. As the philosopher Confucius said, "A journey of a thousand miles begins with a single step." Congratulate yourself for your wins, at any level, and acknowledge your efforts.

Self-Harming Behaviors:

The Actions You Take and the Choices You Make

1 self-harm inventory: you can be a survivor!

for you to know

Pop star Demi Lovato speaks about becoming a survivor of self-harm by saying, "You are beautiful, and you're worth more than harming yourself." As you may know, Demi Lovato and many other pop icons have their struggles with self-harm—cutting, addiction, and other destructive behaviors. Sometimes they are able to overcome them, while at other times, they may have a tougher time. This stuff is not easy by any means, but it is possible to find your way out of the pain and suffering. When you engage in self-harming behaviors, it can be difficult to believe that you're strong and that you can move through and overcome your struggle(s) without hurting yourself. You *can* learn new healthy ways to manage whatever it is you are trying to mask with your self-harming behavior(s), and you *can* get relief from the thoughts and feelings that are leading to you harming yourself.

pain and self-harm

Pain is there for a reason and provides you with information—be it physical or emotional. Noticing, acknowledging, and accepting your physical or emotional pain is *not* the same thing as approving of the events that caused it. The information it provides also doesn't take away from or negate the stress or suffering you have because of your pain. Pain does want to be heard and noticed, but you don't have to do anything to add to or negate your pain. You will learn that you don't have to self-harm to manage your pain.

Self-harm is the way you harm yourself physically or emotionally—with your behaviors, thoughts, and feelings. Although trying to manage or deal with pain using self-harm might seem like a good way to fix your problem, it *will not* fix your problem. It often even makes the problem worse. What's more, the source of that pain will still be there after you have engaged in self-harm. People often don't have the skills or know that there are healthy ways to manage pain and suffering. The activities throughout this book will enable you to manage pain and suffering without self-harm, or at the very least reduce what you might currently be doing.

self-harm inventory

It isn't until you are aware of a behavior that you can then *choose* to stop doing it and *choose* to do something different. Below is an inventory of self-harming behaviors, listed in alphabetical order; you can also download a copy at http://www.newharbinger .com/43676.

When completing this inventory, please take a rigorous, hard look at yourself, and honestly assess what behaviors you are currently engaging in or have used in the past. If you don't feel comfortable marking them for fear that someone might see, take a mental note. If you engage in a behavior that isn't listed, please add it when you get to the spaces listed as *other*, or reflect on it.

Self-Harm Inventory

☐ Being or staying in harmful peer or romantic relationships

☐ Burning

☐ Carving words or symbols on the skin

☐ Cutting (cuts or severe scratches)

☐ Dangerous sexual behaviors (for example, promiscuity)

☐ Embedding objects in your body or under your skin

☐ Head banging

☐ Hitting or punching something (for example, a wall or door)

☐ Ingesting toxic substances or objects

☐ Interfering with a wound that is healing

☐ Making self-harm videos (for example, of cutting or harming yourself)

☐ Neglecting yourself

☐ Picking or scratching your skin

☐ Piercing your skin with sharp objects

☐ Placing excessive trust in people you don't know well

☐ Posting content on social media that is harming to yourself or others

☐ Posting sexual videos or images of yourself

☐ Pulling out your hair

☐ Putting yourself in violent or harmful situations

☐ Unhealthy eating: bingeing, purging, restricting

☐ Using (abusing) drugs or alcohol

☐ Other: _____

☐ Other: _____

☐ Other: _____

This inventory isn't meant to shame you, cause you more pain, or embarrass you. Rather, it is here to provide you with information about what you might be doing that is considered a self-harming behavior. You might not even realize that the way you are trying to cope and manage life is harmful to you. Once you are aware of the self-harming behavior(s) you are using, you can begin to change the behavior and engage in alternative ways of managing and coping with your pain.

mindful takeaway in the moment   When you are aware of a self-harming behavior you are engaging in, you can *choose* to stop doing it and *choose* to engage in healthier behaviors. The choice and power are in your hands.

awareness, now what?

Awareness leads to change. Once you have insight around the types of self-harming behavior(s) you are, or have been, engaging in, you can begin to use behaviors that are healthier for you. First things first.

The upcoming status assessment can pinpoint areas in your life that often trigger you and might need adjusting or changing, as well as areas that are going well that you might be able to turn to as a resource to help you combat the things that aren't working, or when you feel like self-harming. You might find you have a lot to write or very little to provide—either is fine. If you're going through this book on your own, doing this assessment can help you, and if you are working with another person, it can help them to help you.

Answer these questions to the best of your ability. You can jot down notes or write more formally: it's up to you.

What would you like to be different in your life right now?

_____

_____

_____

_____

_____

_____

What in your life *isn't* working well or going the way you would like right now?

_____

_____

_____

_____

_____

_____

What in your life *is* working well and going the way you would like right now?

_____

_____

_____

_____

_____

In the past, were you able to change some things in your life in a positive way? If so, what were they?

_____

_____

_____

_____

_____

_____

2 self-harm awareness calendar: keeping score of self-harm

for you to know

Spiritual leader and peace activist Thich Nhat Hanh beautifully stated, "Awareness is like the sun. When it shines on things, they are transformed." Before you act, be aware; check in with what is going on around you and within you. Tracking your self-harming behaviors is an important step toward doing something different.

the relationship between self-harming behaviors, thoughts, and feelings

Self-harming *behaviors* are recognized and discussed in today's culture more often than self-harming *thoughts* or *feelings*. Self-harming behaviors are generally physical behaviors that someone engages in (for example, cutting or burning) that can leave bodily marks or scars. People often turn to these physical behaviors to numb, or keep at bay, an emotional pain they are having. However, there are more extreme and more serious types of behaviors that can lead to serious physical harm and, even in some extreme cases, death. Self-harming behaviors need to be taken very seriously! Unfortunately, there are times when people engage in these behaviors as a cry for help and are not intending to end their life, but they underestimate the severity of what they are doing—and their actions can still lead to death.

Self-harming behaviors are *more* physically serious than self-harming thoughts or feelings. Self-harming thoughts and feelings are those judgments, emotions, moods, and beliefs someone has about a person, a place, an object, or an event that often precede the self-harming behavior. A self-harming thought might be *I am stupid; I am ugly;* or *I am worthless.* A self-harming feeling might be *I am so sad I can't take this pain anymore. I am going to cut on myself;* or *I feel so angry and irritated all I want to do is isolate in my room and burn myself.* Any one of these thoughts and feelings can lead to the desire to engage in a self-harming behavior to numb the pain it is causing or distract from the emotional pain or feeling someone is having.

People don't often look for, or pay attention to, the thought(s) and feeling(s) that precede the behavior, but there will be one, if not many, cues that lead to the self-harming behavior(s). If you can learn what thought(s) and feeling(s) you are having that trigger you before you engage in a self-harming behavior, you can break the pattern of a harmful thought or feeling leading to a harmful behavior. That is why it is so important to learn about what thoughts you tell yourself and what feelings you have that might be triggering, leading to, or impacting your self-harming behaviors. Harmful thoughts and feelings alone will not leave physical wounds or cause death, but behaviors can.

Note: *Self-harming thoughts and feelings will be discussed in detail in Section 3 of this book.*

becoming more aware of your self-harming behaviors

Self-harming behaviors are Band-Aids or distractions to numb or mask emotional pain by physically hurting yourself. Self-harm makes things worse, not better. After you engage in self-harm, you are still left with the original person, place, object, event, thought, or feeling that led to the behavior in the first place. When you want to engage in one (or more) of the self-harming behaviors you identified in the self-harm inventory in Activity 1, it can be helpful to write down and record what is occurring *before* you engage in the behavior(s).

Remember, awareness can lead to meaningful change:

- You can gain information about what triggers you to want to hurt yourself. You can start to become more aware of the circumstances, environments, people, or things that contribute to your self-harming behavior(s).

- You can give yourself time to think and reflect, to take pause or space, before you do anything. You might decide to do something different.

- You can identify common themes and patterns that are problematic for you and lead to self-harming behavior(s). Maybe you'll learn to make some changes to prevent these areas from becoming problematic for you in the future.

self-harm awareness tracker

Each time you want to engage in a self-harming behavior, follow these steps to complete the Self-Harm Awareness Tracker. At http://www.newharbinger.com/43676, you can download a copy of this form.

Note: *It is not preferred, but you can complete this tracker after you have engaged in a self-harming behavior. If you are completing this after you have harmed yourself, write down what you remember.*

1. List the day of the week, date, and approximate time.

2. Describe the situation. Who is there, what is happening, and where are you?

3. Identify the harmful behavior(s) you feel the urge to engage in. Write it (them) down.

4. Write down any thoughts that arise in the moment.

5. Write down any feelings that come up in the moment.

6. *Pause.* Take a mindful moment before you follow through with the behavior. Now check in with yourself, noticing any physical sensations, thoughts, and feelings. Write down what you want to do after pausing.

7. Write down any new thoughts or feelings that may have come up.

Self-Harm Awareness Tracker

Date and time	Situation (who, what, where)	Harmful behavior(s)	My thought(s) in the moment	My feeling(s) in the moment	After pausing, what I want to do	My new thought(s) or feeling(s)
Monday, around three	Outside school, I overheard two of my friends saying my boyfriend is too good-looking for me.	I want to cut myself. I don't want to eat anymore today.	I'm not pretty. I'm fat. I'm not good enough.	I feel hopeless, sad, insecure, and lonely.	I want to spend some time listening to music that makes me feel uplifted, and call my cousin, who is always supportive.	Cutting or starving myself won't change how I feel or make things better. There are things I love about how I look. I am more than my physical appearance and have a lot to offer. I am still sad, but I am hopeful this will pass. I recognize I am worthy. I accept myself for who I am!

Date and time	Situation (who, what, where)	Harmful behavior(s)	My thought(s) in the moment	My feeling(s) in the moment	After pausing, what I want to do	My new thought(s) or feeling(s)

mindful takeaway in the moment   Remember, your first thought or instinct to do something can often be wrong. Take a minute before you hurt yourself to check in and be aware. Know that you are not alone, and you can always do something different!

self-harm awareness tracker debriefing

When you have completed the rows in this tracker, or after a few weeks to a month's time, think about whether you still have the urge to harm yourself. Ask yourself whether the situation that led you to want to hurt yourself in the first place would change if you engaged in the harming behavior.

What did you observe or learn from completing this tracker?

_____

_____

_____

_____

Did you notice any patterns around people, places, objects, or events that led you to want to harm yourself?

_____

_____

_____

_____

_____

Overall, did you notice any patterns to your thoughts or feelings after completing this tracker?

_____

_____

_____

Are there any changes you already know you can make? If so, write them here.

_____

_____

_____

Information and awareness are very powerful. Once you understand the circumstances surrounding your behaviors and what (or who) triggers you, you can identify patterns; then you can figure out what is within your control to change. For example, maybe you notice after filling out the tracker that you often want to cut yourself after leaving a class where you were bullied or teased. You can start thinking of solutions. Perhaps you create a ritual of listening to a song you like or reading one of your favorite quotes every day before class to remind yourself of who you are and the things you like about yourself. There will be many ideas in this book, so do not be discouraged if you don't have the solutions yet. If you still want to harm yourself right now, after going through this activity, please reach out and talk to a trusted adult or professional.

pain is there for a reason   3

for you to know

As the famous Swiss-American psychiatrist Elisabeth Kübler-Ross said, "The most beautiful people we have known are those who have known defeat, known suffering, known struggle, known loss, and have found their way out of the depths. These persons have an appreciation, a sensitivity, and an understanding of life that fills them with compassion, gentleness, and a deep loving concern." Pain, both physical and emotional, is your body communicating with you, telling you that something is out of balance and needs your attention. Moreover, it presents an opportunity to learn and grow.

the gift of information emotional pain provides

Emotional pain can be more difficult to manage than physical pain because it is harder to describe how it feels. It can also be more challenging to relieve. Emotions describe how we feel inside. People sometimes use physical words to describe them, like "I have a broken heart," or "I'm so mad that I'm shaking," or "My head feels like it's going to explode."

American culture often devalues emotions, especially certain emotions like anxiety, sadness, and anger. People are often taught what they are supposed to feel or how long it is appropriate to feel negative feelings after a painful experience, like the loss of a loved one. It's common to block yourself from expressing feelings that are considered "bad," for fear of being seen as weak, emotionally unstable, immature, or irrational, by yourself or by others. Sometimes you aren't even sure what you are feeling; maybe you just have a felt sense that you can't put into words. Your first reaction might be to numb the emotional pain or distract yourself from it by physically hurting yourself in some way. This isn't the answer!

While some feelings, like anger, loneliness, or jealousy, have a bad rep and are labeled as "negative" or "bad," it can be helpful to notice and acknowledge all feelings as they come and see them as a gift and message to you. Feelings, once noticed, can provide you with a lot of valuable information. Realizing that it's okay to be irritated, to reveal feelings of loneliness or fear—and that it doesn't mean something is wrong with you or define who you are as a person—gives you permission to express whatever you're feeling in that moment. You can then try to figure out what message is being communicated. Emotions provide you with information:

- Anger can bring clarity about your identity (for example, what's important to you—your values and views on things) and your need to create boundaries.

- Fear and anxiety can show you what you need to feel safe, satisfied, supported, and connected, and can help increase your courage and strength.

- Sadness can offer you a gift of healing and give you compassion and connection to other human beings and to yourself.

the gift of information physical pain provides

When you are in pain, it might seem like a good idea to engage in self-harm, but it is far from a good idea. You aren't actually fixing, managing, or dealing with the problem that caused you pain; rather, you are masking it, or possibly even making it worse. For example, if you had a broken leg, you wouldn't put a Band-Aid on it to heal; you would need a cast. If you manage pain with another type of pain—self-harm—you aren't dealing with the root problem. This awareness can be helpful to you when you feel that self-harm is the answer to your painful problem(s). Engaging in self-harm might, in the moment, seem like the best or only option, or the quickest "feel better" tool, but most often it is going to lead to you continuing to feel bad, or even worse, about yourself.

Self-harm causes more pain, self-deprecation, and destruction. It is a vicious cycle that you can get caught up in.

Think of a time when you were physically hurt or injured in some way, whether you fell off your bike or smashed your finger in a door. Describe what the pain actually felt like physically.

_____

_____

Describe what it felt like emotionally (for example, you felt irritated at the door for smashing your finger, you felt scared when you saw the blood, or worried that your might have broken your finger).

_____

_____

_____

What might have happened differently had you not experienced the physical sensation of pain and perhaps didn't even know you had been hurt?

_____

_____

_____

mindful takeaway in the moment   Sometimes a pain just wants to be heard, acknowledged, and recognized. Pain—emotional and physical—is a gift; it may not be pleasant, but all pain is there for a reason. Give yourself permission to honor each pain as it arises before rushing in to fix or change anything. Try to begin to shift your perspective, seeing that a pain is a gift of information.

what a pain!

Experiences of pain can range from mildly unpleasant to downright unbearable. Whatever type—emotional or physical—and however intense the pain is, the first instinct is often to make it go away. However, before you jump in and try to push it away, or find a quick fix to relieve it, you can first acknowledge that it's there for a reason. Think about what your body may be communicating to you. You can use this mindful awareness as an opportunity to learn more about yourself and what you need. This knowledge can allow you to find healthier ways to cope with your pain or distress and to get your needs met.

Think of a situation in which you experienced one of the emotions described in the previous section (anger, fear, anxiety, or sadness).

Who was involved?

_____

What took place?

_____

_____

_____

When did it take place?

_____

_____

Where did it take place?

_____

What emotion(s) did you feel?

_____

_____

How did you react to the situation?

_____

_____

Looking back, what information was this emotion providing you?

_____

_____

_____

_____

_____

_____

To learn more about the complexity of your emotions, go to *Your Feeling IQ* at http://www.newharbinger.com/43676.

4 stress equals pain times blocking (S = P x B)

for you to know

Pain is an inevitable part of the human experience. However, how stressed you become during and after a painful moment depends heavily on what you do in response to it and how you manage it. You can respond in ways that can reduce and manage the pain, or you can react with *blocking behaviors* that often create more stress, wreaking havoc on your mind and body. Blocking behaviors include actions that neither serve you nor help you manage your pain in a healthy, productive, or positive way—although at the time they might seem like the easiest or quickest fix.

blocking behaviors: your band-aids

Below is a list of common blocking behaviors. Circle any you engage in or have engaged in when you experience physical or emotional pain:

Engaging in self-harming behaviors

Pushing the problem or pain away

Socially isolating (pulling the covers over your head in bed to avoid facing the world, for example)

Expressing guilt or shaming yourself about the problem or pain

Minimizing or discounting your own experience or pain (*Other people have it so much worse than I do.*)

Obsessing about the problem or your pain (for example, repeatedly checking your ex's SnapChat account)

Denying that the problem or pain exists

Avoiding the problem or pain by actively avoiding people, places, objects, or events

Resisting the problem

Ignoring the pain your problem causes

Ruminating about it (repeatedly playing a depressing song that makes you feel even worse)

Judging yourself

Telling yourself you should, could, or would have done something different, or asking yourself *Why didn't I do that?*

Noticing your blocking (or unhealthy and harmful coping) behaviors in this list is not meant to shame you, or to have you start mentally beating yourself up. Many people block their pain because they simply don't have more productive ways to positively cope with it. In the coming activities in this book, you will learn ways to positively manage and cope with painful life events. Here is one.

stress equals pain times blocking (S = P x B)

Self-harm and other blocking behaviors add to painful experiences, making them more stressful. Check out Kim's experience to see how the simple equation $S = P \times B$ can apply to all painful experiences.

Painful experience: *Kim's boyfriend of six months broke up with her yesterday, saying, "There's just something missing."*

Type of pain: *Emotional. Kim is sad, hurt, lonely, and confused. She didn't see it coming and is wondering what she did wrong, what he feels is "missing," and why she isn't "good enough" for him. She thought they would be together forever and assumed he felt the same.*

Pain rating (on a scale of 0–100; 0 is no pain at all, 100 is unbearable pain): *Kim describes her emotional pain as 100.*

Blocking behaviors: *Yikes. After going through the list above, Kim realizes that she's (1) socially isolating by staying home from school and not coming out of her room; (2) pushing the problem away; (3) ruminating over the problem by continually thinking about him and their relationship and replaying "their song" on her iPhone; (4) blaming herself for doing something to push him away; (5) obsessing over the problem by constantly checking his social media and looking at her phone, waiting for him to contact her and change his mind; (6) judging herself for not being "good enough" for him; (7) engaging in unhealthy coping behaviors by restricting her food and sneaking her mom's prescription of antianxiety meds.*

Blocking rating (on a scale of 0–100; 0 is no blocking, 100 is a ton of blocking): *Kim rates her blocking at 80.*

After Kim charts her pain and blocking to connect the two [P (100) x B (80)], she realizes she is experiencing 8,000 units of stress.

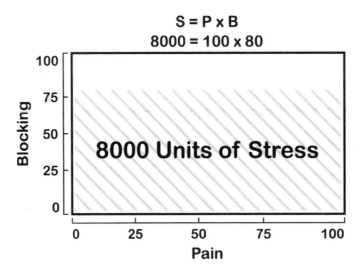

With this realization, Kim makes some changes to gain control of and lower her stress. Her pain hasn't gone down; she still gives it a rating of 100, but she lowers her blocking behaviors from 80 to 40 by doing the following: *(1) reaching out to friends and no longer socially isolating; (2) trying not to blame herself for the breakup; (3) deleting her former boyfriend from social media and her phone contacts so she won't keep checking up on him; (4) eating more balanced, healthy meals again and no longer taking her mom's meds.*

Here is her new chart, with the same experience level of pain, but fewer blocking behaviors:

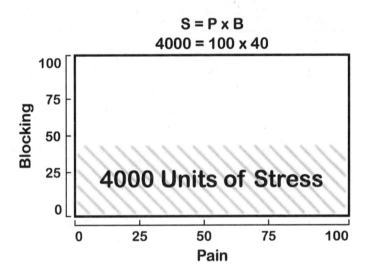

Kim significantly improved her overall mood and health by reducing her blocking behaviors and lowering her experience of stress. She has taken some important steps to move in a healthier direction.

mindful takeaway in the moment   Pain is inevitable; stress is optional. As Viktor Frankl, Holocaust survivor and existential psychologist, eloquently stated, "Forces beyond your control can take everything you possess except one thing: your freedom to choose how you respond to the situation."

managing your pain

List up to five emotional or physical pains you are experiencing in your life.

1. _____

2. _____

3. _____

4. _____

5. _____

Following Kim's example, pick one pain from this list that is currently causing you stress.

Painful experience: Describe the person, place, object, or event causing you pain.

_____

_____

_____

Type of pain: Describe the kind of pain you are experiencing.

_____

_____

Pain rating (on a scale of 0–100; 0 is no pain at all, 100 is unbearable pain):

_____

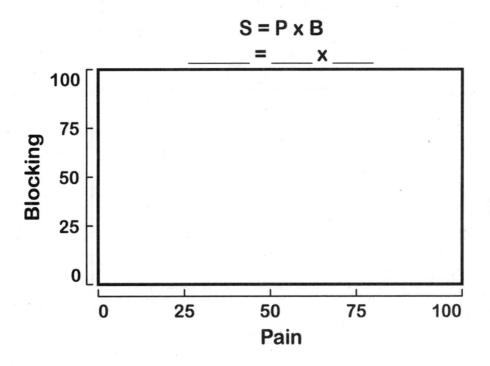

Blocking behaviors: List your blocking behaviors, referring to the list above to help as needed.

_____

_____

_____

_____

Blocking rating (on a scale of 0–100; 0 is no blocking, 100 is a ton of blocking):

_____

Use this chart to plot how stressed you are. At http://www.newharbinger.com/43676, you can download a blank version.

S = P x B

_____ = _____ x _____

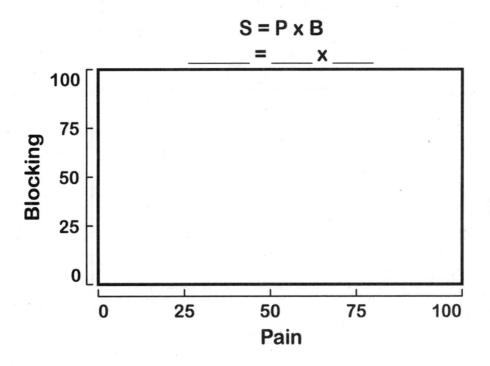

Even if the pain stayed the same number, what blocking behaviors could you change, reduce, or eliminate? (Refer to the list of blocking behaviors above to help you.)

_____

_____

_____

_____

After making these changes (or imagining that you have made, or will make them), rate your blocking again.

_____

Use this blank chart to plot how stressed you are after you change some of your blocking behaviors.

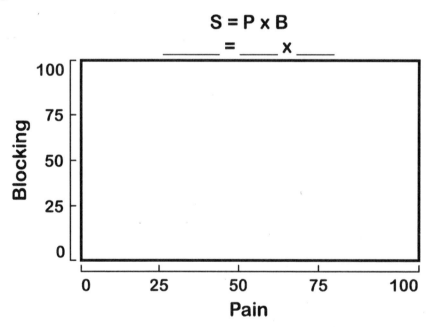

Compare the two diagrams and see how you can change your stress level by changing, reducing, or eliminating some (or all) of your blocking behaviors.

responding to stress: the fight-flight-or-freeze response

5

for you to know

Way, way back in the day, our ancestors had to be ready at a moment's notice to either confront or flee from predators like saber-toothed tigers. The fight-or-flight response was essential to their survival!

In the same way, your body's stress response prepares you to immediately deal with threatening situations. Say you are camping and hear a bear roar in the distance. A small almond-shaped part of your brain called the *amygdala*, considered the emotional center of your brain, fires up. It detects fear and responds to anything perceived as an emergency or a threat. Your amygdala then communicates this perception to your nervous system (the part called the *sympathetic nervous system*, or SNS for short, which helps you react to stress and danger) and triggers a host of reactions throughout your body: your pupils may dilate to help you see more sharply, your heartbeat may speed up to prepare you to fight or flee, your breath might become quick and shallow.

In addition to fight-or-flight, there is another type of response that has been talked about more recently—kind of like a deer in headlights—the freeze response. Your brain is hardwired to keep you safe, and the fight-flight-or-freeze response can be helpful in a variety of situations, but it can also cause or exacerbate physical and emotional pain. In turn, you might experience the fight-flight-or-freeze response and automatically turn to a self-harming behavior. It is imperative if you are in one of these response states to first recognize it, then take a brief pause if you feel like you are going to engage in self-harm. This brief pause may stop you from reacting with a self-harming behavior.

To learn more about the fight-flight-or-freeze response, go to *Fight-Flight-or-Freeze Response in Your Body* in the online resources section at http://www.newharbinger .com/43676.

assess your response to stress

This table lists many common physical and emotional symptoms that arise when the fight-flight-or-freeze response is engaged. Circle any that apply or have applied to you in a stressful or painful situation. Now star any that may have triggered you to engage in self-harming behaviors.

Note: *You might experience these symptoms during responses other than the one they are listed under.*

Fight response	Flight response	Freeze response
PHYSICAL • Feeling hot, warm, or sweaty • Clenched jaw or fists • Knotted or upset stomach EMOTIONAL • Feelings of anger or rage • Desire to punch, kick, stomp, or break something • Crying • Homicidal or suicidal thoughts	• Restlessness • Shallow, rapid breathing • Feeling trapped • Crying • Fidgety • Rapid, darting eye movement • Anxiety • Butterflies in stomach	• Feeling cold, frozen, or numb • Tightness in chest • Difficulty breathing • Crying • Paralysis or difficulty moving • Sense of dread • Pounding heart

Which of the physical symptoms listed have you experienced? Write them here, and add any others you've experienced that are similar.

_____

_____

_____

Which of the emotional symptoms listed have you experienced? Write them here, and add any others you've experienced.

_____

_____

_____

_____

Now that you know that the symptoms you starred are triggered by the fight-flight-or-freeze response, you can remind yourself that you don't have to engage in a self-harming behavior because you feel one or more of these symptoms.

mindful takeaway in the moment   The fight-flight-or-freeze response provides red flags that can help you protect yourself in stressful or dangerous situations. When you are in one of these states, you don't have to self-harm; just notice the physical and emotional symptoms and know that *they will pass*.

when the fight-flight-or-freeze response doesn't help you

The fight-flight-or-freeze response gets activated in many situations where it isn't needed or helpful. Your body reacts to most stressful moments in your life, ranging from things like a picture posted on social media to a loud bang on your door, with the same fight-flight-or-freeze response as if you were encountering a tiger. The problem arises when the amygdala is in overdrive or not working properly. People may perceive situations or other people as threats to their safety—often due to past traumas—when they may not be unsafe or in danger at all.

Neuropsychologist Rick Hanson has described this phenomenon as *paper tiger paranoia*, meaning that people often react to a "paper" tiger as though it were a real tiger. Your body responds to life stressors, these paper tigers, all the time, and you feel the effects mentally and physically as if you were encountering a real tiger every day, perhaps even many times a day. Once you tune into your body and learn to identify these paper tigers, you can determine whether there is, in fact, a real threat and take the time to mindfully reflect on how you can best avoid self-harm.

Write about a time when your body's fight-flight-or-freeze response to a stressful situation or threat *was* helpful in the moment. Describe what happened, how you felt in your body, and how it helped you cope.

_____

_____

_____

_____

Write about a time when your body's fight-flight-or-freeze response *was not* helpful in the moment. Describe what happened, how you felt in your body, and how it did *not* help you cope.

_____

_____

_____

_____

When you are in a fight-flight-or-freeze response, the activities that follow can help you with healthy ways to cope with and manage your symptoms.

grounding yourself when you are in pain 6

for you to know

Well-known writer Michael Gruber said, "It turns out that people who are grounded and secure don't change much under stress. That's what being grounded means." Everyone experiences stress and pain, and at times the fight-flight-or-freeze response gets triggered. If you can ground yourself during painful times, it can (1) help shift you out of or away from a difficult emotional or physical state; (2) be a calming function—something to turn to when you are in pain, stressed, or wanting to harm yourself; and (3) actually ground you if you are experiencing the fight-flight-or-freeze response.

grounding focal points

Grounding focal points are physical or functional parts of the body that are always with you. They can be turned to and noticed at any time and used to bring you into the present moment. Your feet and hands are two grounding focal points you can turn to at any moment. Focusing on these points can help shift you out of or away from a difficult emotional state, and at times help you tune into your pain instead of blocking it with self-harm.

grounding yourself: a practice

Here are some examples of grounding with your *feet*:

- Walking barefoot on surfaces such as grass, sand, or carpet

- Putting your feet in cold running water in the tub

- Walking with shoes on surfaces such as dirt, wood, or tile

- Noticing what is surrounding or on your feet (for example, shoes, socks)

- Noticing each of your toes

- Wiggling each of your toes

Choose three of these and do them right now. List your choices here:

_____   _____   _____

After grounding yourself using your feet, what did you notice?

_____

_____

_____

Here are some examples of grounding with your *hands*:

- Holding an ice cube in your hand until it melts

- Putting your hand in or under cold running water

- Noticing the air or sensations on or around your hands

- Observing each of your hands

- Touching a single finger to your thumb

- Counting your fingers

- Observing each of your fingers

- Wiggling your fingers

Choose three of these and do them right now. List your choices here:

_____   _____   _____

After grounding yourself using your hands, what did you notice?

_____

_____

_____

You can use these grounding techniques when you are feeling the urge to self-harm.

mindful takeaway in the moment   When you become aware of and notice signs and cues that you are experiencing pain or distress—for example, the fight-flight-or-freeze response is triggered—you can use your feet or hands to literally ground you to the present moment and prevent your pain from escalating.

personalize your grounding focal points

Marcus wears a rubber band on his right wrist, and when he feels upset and is considering harming himself, he snaps the rubber band against his wrist a few times. He feels some sting from the snapping. Doing this helps bring him back from his thoughts and into the present moment. He has learned that he doesn't have to engage in self-harm to feel physical sensations and go down the numbing path that he was often doing with scratching on himself.

Sherri rubs her favorite lotion on her fingers and hands. She uses her thumb and forefinger to put some pressure on the spots of her hand that are tight. Noticing her hands and not the to-do list in her head helps her feel relief from the tightness and be in the present moment.

What are five ways that you can think of to ground yourself? List them here:

1. _____

2. _____

3. _____

4. _____

5. _____

When you are feeling stressed, your fight-flight-or-freeze response is starting to be triggered, or you want to engage in self-harm, remember to turn to any of the grounding focal points you chose.

negative coping behaviors and positive coping skills

7

for you to know

Some ways of coping with pain and stress are healthy and helpful, while others are unhealthy and harmful. People who tend to rely on self-harming behaviors, thoughts, and feelings often cope by doing things that are unhelpful, thinking it will solve their problems or make them feel better—because that is what they know. Unfortunately, they find afterward that this generally makes them feel worse overall. Learning new positive skills to cope can help you fight back tendencies to turn to negative coping behaviors. A *negative coping behavior* is something people turn to and engage in that might appear to help the problem or pain, but it doesn't. That is why it is called a behavior and not a skill: because it is not useful in solving problems or easing pains.

Positive coping skills are actions you can engage in that can ease your problems and pain and hopefully make you feel better.

negative coping behaviors

Negative coping behaviors include the following:

- Alcohol use and abuse

- Drug use and abuse (including improper use of prescription drugs)

- Sleeping too much or not enough

- Stealing

- Hoarding

- Hanging out with people who are unhealthy or toxic for you

- Getting into fights

- Drinking a lot of caffeine or energy drinks

- Isolating yourself by staying in your room

- Turning down plans

- Spending less time with people who nourish or support you

- Not doing things you used to like

- Smoking cigarettes or vaping

- Cutting or burning yourself

- Having unprotected sex

- Overeating; bingeing

- Undereating; restricting or withholding food

- Making yourself vomit after eating; purging

- Exercising excessively

- Spending too much time distracting yourself online or on your phone

Circle any of the negative coping behaviors you are or have been engaging in.

Consider what emotions, pain, or discomfort you may have been trying to cover up with these negative coping behaviors. Use the journal pages in the back of the book to write about any thoughts, feelings, or aha moments that arise from reflecting on these negative coping behaviors. Remember, there is no need to blame yourself or feel shame. This process is to help you be more aware, to learn, and to grow.

mindful takeaway in the moment   People often try to deal with pain by doing things that make them feel worse—negative coping behaviors. It's important to gain awareness of the ways in which you try to cope with pain and to replace negative coping behaviors with positive coping skills.

positive coping skills

Positive coping skills include the following:

- Writing/journaling

- Playing or listening to music

- Drawing/arts and crafts

- Taking a bath

- Playing a sport

- Dancing

- Mindfulness practice

- Talking to or spending time with friends or family

- Going on a walk or hike

- Spending time in nature

- Spending time with an animal

- Taking a dog for a walk

- Other: _____

- Other: _____

- Other: _____

Circle any of these you have engaged in over the past two months or could start to do. On the blank lines, add others you can think of.

How can learning about these positive coping skills help you better listen to or manage the distressful feelings or emotional pains you experience?

_____

_____

_____

_____

Pick one or more of these skills that you can do the next time you feel stressed, are in physical or emotional pain, or feel triggered to self-harm. Write it (them) down here.

_____

_____

_____

letting go is a process that is possible

8

for you to know

"Let come what comes. Let go what goes. See what remains." This quote by Ramana Maharshi, a Hindu sage and spiritual teacher, can be applied to many, if not all, situations, experiences, relationships, and feelings. Letting go can be explained as a process of releasing, lessening, or removing the weight—the emotional and physical pain—something has on you; in this case self-harm. Letting go is a process of taking away the *power* that people, places, objects, or events have over you. Letting go can bring a powerful sense of freedom and clarity into your life. Letting go does not imply forgiveness, or that a situation or an event didn't take place. It isn't the same thing as giving up, giving in, or forgiving someone who has hurt you. Instead, letting go is something done *only for you*, for your own personal benefit. In this activity, the focus is on letting go of the pain you have caused yourself.

letting go of the pain you have caused yourself

If you have engaged in self-harming behaviors, it is crucial that you work on letting go of the pain you have inflicted on yourself—both physical and emotional. In addition to the possible physical scars self-harming behaviors can cause, they can also cause mental scars. You can't necessarily erase the physical scars, but you can work on repairing and lessening the mental ones.

It can be very easy to beat yourself up for hurting yourself. Thoughts like *Why did I do it again? I said I wasn't going to* or *I am worthless* might be commonplace. Over time, these thoughts, and others like them, create deep mental scars that need to be addressed, as they can mentally weigh you down.

When you start to unpack the effects self-harming has on you, some of the mental scars might surface in the form of guilt, shame, blame, or other such conflicted thoughts and feelings. For self-harmers, a personal letting go of what you have done in the past and freeing yourself of the possible guilt and shame can help you heal and move past the effects of self-harm.

let go of your pain: one step at a time

The first step toward being a survivor of self-harm is the willingness to explore how self-harm has impacted you and consider letting go some of the pain you have caused yourself—physically and mentally. This isn't going to happen overnight but being willing is half the battle.

Letting go can allow you to see the experience and your pain for what it is; to sit with it for a brief minute rather than avoid it, push it away, or cling to it for hours on end; and then literally to consider letting it go, allowing you to break the hold it has over you.

It's like saying, "Yep, that experience hurt me; it is something that happened to me. It is part of my story, but it does not control or define me. This is how it made me feel … this is what I can learn from it … and now I am going to let it go and move forward."

letting go in action

Try the process of letting go. Think about a time when you engaged in self-harm. In the space below, provide as much context as you can that led to you self-harming—any information about the people, places, objects, or events that were involved will help make this a more meaningful and useful experience for you.

Write about it here.

_____

_____

_____

_____

_____

_____

_____

_____

Now work on the process of letting go of the pain you have caused yourself, using these steps:

Step 1: Notice your thoughts and feelings.

You can witness thoughts or emotions as if you are watching them from a distance instead of them being part of you. Don't try to push them away or judge what arises; just accept the thoughts as thoughts and the feelings as feelings as they are in this moment. Experience what you think and feel like a wave, rolling in and out, coming and going. Know that these thoughts and feelings, like waves, will pass.

Ask yourself these questions and just observe whatever thought(s) or emotion(s) surface:

What thought(s) or feeling(s) are present right now?

_____

_____

_____

When you think about what you want to let go of, how do you feel?

_____

_____

_____

What thoughts or feelings arise when you consider your willingness to let go of the pain this caused you?

_____

_____

_____

Step 2: Acknowledge what occurred.

Acknowledge to yourself that this is something that happened to you, and acknowledge the thought(s) and feeling(s) you just identified. Remember, you are not your thoughts or feelings—you don't need to do anything about them. This doesn't mean you are saying that what happened is okay, right, or good, or that you deserved the pain or annoyance it may have caused. It's just recognizing that it happened, seeing it for what it is (which often makes the weight you've attached to it become a lot lighter), and taking away some of the power it has had over your thoughts, feelings, and behaviors.

Step 3: Be willing to accept what occurred.

Be willing to accept what truths there are to be had. What are the thoughts and feelings around this person, place, object, or event that are true, real, and factual? What parts are things that may have been added onto it, like worries, judgments, ruminations, and the like? Separate out the fact from the fiction and accept what is just as it is. Be willing to let go of the pain you have felt.

Step 4: Begin to let the pain go.

Everyone deserves to let go of pain. You don't have to hold on to it. You don't have to punish yourself anymore.

Begin to let go of the thoughts or feelings you have held so closely or tightly. Ask yourself whether this person, place, object, or event has become part of your story, part of who you are. Are you stuck on thinking about, clinging to, or holding on to this just a little too much? Know that what took place did, in fact, happen and that you don't have to cling or hold on to related pain, stress, or suffering if you no longer want to. Make the decision to let go. Maybe even say out loud, or write down, something kind to it, as you would tell a close friend, and then let it go with something like, "I release you," or "I am letting go of the hold you've had over me."

This step of letting something go, along with the previous steps, is a lifelong process. No one does these steps perfectly all the time. Sometimes just noticing is a good first step. You can also choose to instead put your focus on doing things that fill you up and serve you. Your willingness to explore even letting go is a significant first step toward change and toward moving through your past.

mindful takeaway in the moment   Letting go helps you regain control over how you think and feel, and thus how you act; it takes away the control your thoughts and feelings have over you and the energy you've spent trying to push them away or change them. Doing this puts you back in the driver's seat. Remember the four steps to letting go: notice, acknowledge, be willing to accept, and begin to let go.

letting go brainstorm

People can develop a relationship with any addiction—using drugs, eating problems, cutting, and so on—that is unhealthy and often extremely toxic. The addiction becomes part of them. Even uber-unhealthy relationships can be hard, and scary, to let go of.

However, when you are able to say good-bye to a toxic relationship with something like a behavior that harms you in some way, you free up space to enter into other relationships that fill you up, support you, and nourish you. What if you could let go of the hold your thoughts and emotions have over you, and let go of your self-harming behaviors as well?

On the lines that follow, brainstorm the people, places, objects, events, or anything else that comes to mind that you would like to work on letting go. By the act of writing them down here, they are no longer secrets to hold on to or keep inside. You can put them here and temporarily let go of the hold they have on you.

List ten things you would like to let go. If you come up with less than ten, that is fine; if you come up with more than ten, continue your list on a separate piece of paper.

1. _____

2. _____

3. _____

4. _____

5. _____

6. _____

7. _____

8. _____

9. _____

10. _____

Be Mindful, Not Harmful:

Mindfulness Practices to Replace Self-Harming Behaviors

9 sense awareness:
a mindfulness practice

for you to know

Actor and comedian Jim Carrey commented about mindfulness in an interview: "If you aren't in the moment, you are either looking forward to uncertainty, or back to pain and regret." Mindfulness is a buzzword getting lots of attention in all kinds of industries, from business to education to professional athletics.

Mindfulness is noticing your thoughts, feelings, and physical sensations in the present moment without harmful judgment. You are mindful when you:

pay attention to what you feel physically;

notice what you are thinking and/or feeling;

are aware of what is around you;

tune into any of your five senses;

are present to yourself and in interactions with others;

are aware of your environment.

When you are mindful, you are more able to make thoughtful and responsive decisions. You become more aware and can choose to respond to what is going on with you physically and mentally rather than reacting with self-harming behaviors, thoughts, or feelings. Mindfulness allows you the space to observe, take a pause, and choose a different, healthier response.

mindful sense awareness practice

At its essence, *mindfulness* is about noticing what is taking place in the present moment—as it is occurring. *Sense awareness* is about being aware of and noticing any or all of your senses. When you pay attention to any of your five senses (sight, smell, taste, sound, touch), congratulations! You are already being mindful.

Let's start with a mindful sense awareness practice noticing your five senses.

What do you *see*? What is in front of you? What is behind you?

_____

_____

_____

What do you *smell*? Now close your eyes. Did you smell anything different?

_____

_____

_____

What do you *taste*? Can you taste the air? The remnants of what you last ate?

_____

_____

_____

What do you *hear*? Again, you might want to close your eyes to sharpen your sense.

_____

_____

_____

What do you *touch*? Your clothes against your skin? A breeze? Your feet on the ground?

_____

_____

_____

Begin to regularly pay attention to and notice any or all of your five senses to anything you are doing—walking, eating, listening to music. If you are paying attention to a sense, you are in the present and less likely to be focused on the past or future.

To learn about other senses beyond the traditional five, go to *Super Senses: Beyond the Big Five* in the online resources section at http://www.newharbinger.com/43676.

mindful takeaway in the moment Sense awareness is one way to be mindful—to notice and be aware of any or all of your five senses (sight, smell, taste, sound, touch). When you are paying attention to any of your senses, you are less likely to engage in self-harm. Sense awareness helps prevent and keep you from being on automatic pilot, numb, or spaced out—states of mind when you are more vulnerable to self-harm.

being mindful of your senses
is not always easy

Being mindful of your senses can be hard for several reasons:

You don't want to feel something.

You don't want to deal with what is going on right now.

You want to escape.

You feel overwhelmed.

You want to be checked out.

List any people, places, objects, or events where you tend to want to be numb, zone or tune out, escape from, or check out of:

_____

_____

_____

_____

_____

_____

It can be hard to tune into what is going on in your body, but being aware of your senses can help you create space to observe, then pause before reacting in many situations.

10 mindful check-in: your highs and lows

for you to know

Virginia Woolf, a noted writer of her time, said, "Without self-awareness we are as babies in a cradle." Have you ever had a headache and not noticed it? Have you ever walked to class and not noticed how you got there? Have you ever been looking for your phone and realized it was already on your person?

The body and mind provide you with useful information, cues, and red flags that want to be noticed. There is value in checking in with yourself so that you don't "wreck" or harm yourself. You can learn how to *check in* with yourself—to know how you are doing, to help you grow, to help point you to areas where things aren't okay, and to let you know which areas are working right. Getting into a routine of frequently checking in is important in maintaining health, happiness, and balance.

mindful check-in

Awareness is the first step toward creating change in your behaviors. To be mindful is to be *aware*—this includes being aware of your senses, but it is much more than sense awareness. Mindful awareness is also about checking in with yourself daily to assess how you are doing—physically and mentally. Just like you charge a phone that is running low or fill a car with gas that is on empty, you need to check in with your gauges that let you know you are physically and mentally okay.

Right now, check in with how you are doing *physically*:

What parts of your body feel healthy?

What parts of your body, if any, are in pain?

What physical sensations do you notice?

What temperature do you feel?

Right now, check in with how you are doing *mentally*:

What thoughts do you have right now?

What mood are you in?

What feelings do you feel?

These are some basic questions to get at how you are doing. You can ask yourself these questions any time you want to check in with yourself. Another way to check in with your mood and how you are doing from day-to-day is to get in the habit of checking in on your highs and lows.

highs and lows

It can be useful to start tracking your highs and lows each day to learn about what fills you up and nourishes you—your *highs*—and what drains and depletes you—your *lows*. You can download this tracker at http://www.newharbinger.com/43676.

Each day this week, list at least one thing you consider a high and one thing you consider a low. Feel free to write more, but it is suggested that you include at least one, if possible.

Highs and Lows

Day of the week	High	Low
Sara's example:	Lindsey told me she feels that she can trust me and that she appreciates my friendship.	Tom, one of the jerk guys at school, told me I was "a bit thick."
Monday		
Tuesday		
Wednesday		
Thursday		
Friday		
Saturday		
Sunday		

mindful takeaway in the moment   Mindful check-ins help you assess how you are doing physically and mentally and reflect on your high(s) and low(s) for the day. Doing this check-in provides you with valuable information to learn more about what your self-harm triggers are.

red flags: finding your self-harm triggers

Sara wanted to cut herself when she got home from school. When Sara considered her high and low for that day, she was better able to understand how her low led her to wanting to hurt herself. She realized that she forgot about the high, the compliment her friend gave her, and that she was focusing only on the low.

In addition to noticing your high(s) and low(s), you can dig deeper and find out what in your life is triggering your self-harming behaviors, thoughts, and feelings. These things are important to check in on so you can learn how to do something different and change your self-harm.

People

Sara's example: *Tom*

List the *people* in your life who tend to be draining, harming, or negative to you.

_____

_____

_____

Places

Sara's example: *In the hall by my locker with Tom.*

List the *places* in your life that tend to be draining, harming, or negative for you.

_____

_____

_____

Objects

Sara's example: *I keep going to check my phone to see if Tom wrote any negative comments about me on social.*

List the *objects* in your life that tend to be draining, harming, or negative for you.

_____

_____

_____

_____

Situations

Sara's example: *I wonder who else thinks I am fat or has been saying things like this behind my back.*

List the *situations* in your life that tend to be draining, harming, or negative for you.

_____

_____

_____

_____

connecting your lows to your red flags

Now that you are more aware of what things have been impacting you, go back to your highs and lows chart and match your lows with the people, places, objects, and/ or situations that were involved. Doing this will help you connect the dots and tie your triggers to your real-life lows by noticing patterns that arise. Learning to make connections between your lows and your red-flag triggers takes time and works.

11 riding the waves: pain will pass

for you to know

Mindfulness teacher and stress reduction expert Jon Kabat-Zinn wrote, "There are always waves on the water. Sometimes they are big, sometimes they are small, and sometimes they are almost imperceptible. The water's waves are churned up by the winds, which come and go and vary in direction and intensity, just as do the winds of stress and change in our lives, which stir up the waves in our minds." Physical or emotional pain causes you to experience stress. The intensity of the stress varies, but nonetheless pain causes you to feel stressed. Imagine that stress can be viewed as waves in the ocean: many stressors, many waves; few stressors, few waves. Just as you can't stop waves from coming, you can't stop stress from coming, or the urges to harm yourself from coming, but how you manage the stress or the urges—making alternative choices and not harming yourself—is the way to manage or ride the waves.

learning about your stress waves helps prevent self-harm

People often engage in self-harm when they are in pain and stressed out. Learning about what stressors you have and how much pain each is causing you can help prevent self-harming thoughts and feelings from becoming behaviors.

Imagine that you are in a rowboat in the ocean. The waves around you represent whatever is causing you stress: the people, places, objects, and events that are affecting you, are your *stress waves*. The waves might be calm and still, or crashing, fierce, and rough. If you have many waves, this means you have a lot of stress and many stressors in your life right now. Think for a minute about what is causing you pain and stressing you out right now. Imagine translating these into waves.

In the rectangle provided below, draw a picture of what your stress waves look like right now. Label the waves with the self-harming behaviors you engage in, the self-harming thoughts or feelings you have, and whatever is stressing you or causing you pain, worry, fear, and the like.

Your Stress Waves

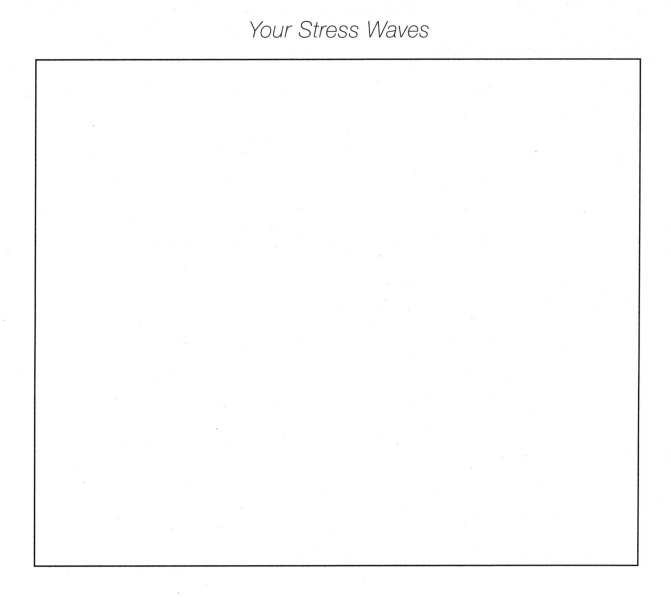

interpreting your stress waves

Describe what you notice about your waves: their size, how many there are, how you drew them, and so on.

_____

_____

What self-harming behaviors did you list?

_____

_____

What self-harming thoughts did you list?

_____

_____

What self-harming feelings did you list?

_____

_____

What people are causing you pain and stress?

_____

_____

What places are causing you pain and stress?

_____

_____

What objects are causing you pain and stress?

_____

_____

What events are causing you pain and stress?

_____

_____

What thoughts come up for you when you look at your drawing and what you wrote?

_____

_____

What feelings come up for you when you look at your drawing and what you wrote?

_____

_____

What, if anything, strikes you about what you wrote or how you drew your waves?

_____

_____

Describe any patterns or areas that stand out to you.

_____

_____

mindful takeaway in the moment   Like waves, your pains and stressors will pass. Sometimes pain and stress will feel like a tsunami; hopefully at other times there will be no waves in sight. Remember that every moment is a new moment, and it too will pass.

take control: managing your stress waves without self-harm

Many people who self-harm say it gives them a sense of power and control over what they are doing and when they are doing it. Often the emotional or physical pain they are experiencing feels so intolerable, unbearable, or out of their control that self-harm seems like a good option because they are then deciding how much pain they cause themselves, and when. What these people haven't learned is that there are healthy ways to manage difficult pains and stressors. Even if you have many pains and stressors, you can get control over them and work toward managing them.

Look back at the stress waves you drew earlier. Which of these are out of your control—meaning that you can't change them no matter what you do? Draw a line through these.

List the waves you have no control over.

_____

_____

_____

_____

_____

List the waves that require the action of others. Draw a squiggly line through these.

_____

_____

_____

_____

_____

Which are more long-term waves (three to six months)? Draw an X through these.

List the long-term waves.

_____

_____

_____

_____

_____

Right now, you can begin to work on the remaining pains and stressors, those that have no marking through them. It isn't that the rest of these don't need fixing or to be worked on, but having success managing the pains and stressors that are within your control and ability to change is a great start. Experiencing incremental successes when managing and dealing with your problems is often going to lead you to feel a sense of control and perhaps motivate you to do more. Success breeds success!

12 finding your anchor: a grounding practice

for you to know

Imagine yourself in a rowboat. Notice the stress waves around you, and imagine dropping an anchor from your boat to the ocean floor. Even when the waves are like a tsunami on the surface, if you follow this anchor down deep to the floor of the ocean, the water is often calm and still. You have learned about your grounding focal points and ways to focus on the stress waves you do have control over. Now you will learn a mindfulness practice to anchor yourself when you are in pain; feeling stressed, overwhelmed, or out of control; or want to harm yourself.

mindful anchoring practice

Before you begin this mindful anchoring practice, turn to the first journal page at the back of this book or use a separate piece of paper, and write down what you are thinking, how you are feeling, and what pains or stressors are present; then return to this activity.

Now, to the best of your ability, set aside whatever you wrote down, and put your focus and attention on this practice.

Follow these eight steps to anchor yourself to this moment, to help get you to a calm, still place—physically and mentally.

Step 1: Location Awareness

  Notice the time of day (ex: morning, night).

  Notice where you are (ex: home, school).

Step 2: Mind Awareness

Notice what thoughts are here.

Notice what feelings are here.

Notice your mood.

Step 3: Awareness of Your Surroundings

Take in your surroundings. Notice what is here to be noticed with your senses (sight, smell, taste, sound, touch).

Step 4: Body Awareness

Notice your energy level (ex: tired, awake).

Notice the position of your body (ex: sitting, standing, lying down).

Notice the points of contact your body has with the surface you are on.

Let go of any facial expression you might be holding.

Let go of any clenching in your jaw.

Release any muscles that might be tight or tense (ex: shoulders).

Notice any physical sensations that are present from the tips of your toes to the top of your head.

Step 5: Sense of Touch: Hands and Feet

Wiggle your toes.

Notice what is on or surrounding your feet.

Touch the ground with your feet.

Wiggle your fingers.

Touch each of your fingers to your thumbs one at a time.

Notice the air between your fingers and on and around your hands.

Touch your clothes or some object near your person.

Step 6: Breathing Through

Imagine there is a small blowhole at the top of your head, like that of a dolphin. Breathe in through the top of your head, moving this in-breath all the way through your body and releasing it out through the tips of your toes. Repeat two or three times as needed for calm and relaxation.

Step 7: Detective Station

After you have followed your breathing a few times from the top of your head through the tips of your toes, what pains, if any, did you notice?

Did you notice anything familiar?

Did you notice anything new?

Take another breath and breathe into any areas you choose, bringing in cool, calm, clean air. On your next out-breath, release any tension, tightness, pain, or stress you wish to let go of.

Step 8: Being Your Anchor: Let Go

You have the power at any moment to let go of anything that is holding you back—that is preventing you from anchoring yourself. If there is anything you would you like to let go of, consider it now.

After completing this practice, how do you feel?

_____

_____

What thoughts or feelings are present for you?

_____

_____

_____

Remember, you can repeat this process at any time to help anchor you to the present moment. This practice can help you drop below the stress waves on the surface of the water to find your calm, still, quiet place. In the future, you can do this practice quickly or slowly; you might choose to skip a few points under each of the eight steps, depending on the time you have available. There is no need to go back to what you wrote, but if you find there might be some insights in reviewing it after you have done this practice, feel free to do so.

mindful takeaway in the moment   Even if stress waves are around you, at any time you can choose to drop your anchor and get to your calm, still, quiet place below the surface of the water. You can always use the mindful anchoring practice if you are wanting to engage in self-harm.

flip the script

You have been asked a few times to think of the people, places, objects, and events that are the source of, or negative influence on, your pain, stress, and self-harming behaviors. This time, flip the script: In the image of the anchor below, list the things that help calm, ground, and anchor you. These can be anything that positively impacts you in a healthy way and that supports the survivor in you.

befriending your body: 13
the body scan
mindfulness practice

for you to know

Eckhart Tolle, a best-selling author and spiritual teacher, said, "Body awareness not only anchors you in the present moment … it also strengthens the immune system and the body's ability to heal itself." Often you are aware of how you feel in your body only right after some uncomfortable sensation has come up and you are trying to avoid or relieve it. For example, your stomach growls, signaling that you are hungry, so you eat. Your nose itches, so you scratch it. Humans possess the unique ability of self-awareness: taking a step back and observing themselves.

One way to be self-aware is to do the body scan mindfulness practice. This practice is about being a detective or a tourist who is sightseeing through all the regions of your body. You tune in and notice what is going on in your body without trying to change anything you notice. The body scan is also a great alternative to do instead of, or before, engaging in self-harming behaviors. You can also use this practice to help you when you are experiencing the fight-flight-or-freeze response or if you notice feelings such as anxiety, depression, fear, or anger coming up or starting to become overwhelming.

befriend, don't betray, your body

If you engage in self-harming behaviors, you are betraying your body—you aren't honoring your pain, and you are damaging and destroying your body in some way. The body scan practice can help you befriend your body and honor your pain by being with and checking into it. When you feel pain, you can notice it before doing something that is harming. Awareness is key to being mindful, and the body scan is about becoming aware of your body just as it is right now.

This practice, like other mindfulness practices in this book, can be used *instead* of self-harming. The body scan practice can help you:

become aware of your body;

pause and tune into your body;

pay attention to the physical sensations and information your body is providing (for example, headache, tight chest, tingling in your fingers);

take a pause before you engage in self-harm.

By bringing awareness to some or all parts of your body, you are less likely to be focused on your self-harming physical urges, or on thoughts that are tied up in the past or future; instead, you are more in the now. This practice can calm you physically and emotionally and alleviate the feelings that trigger your urge to hurt yourself in some way.

preparing for the body scan mindfulness practice

Start by finding a comfortable place, free from as many distractions as possible. You can set a timer for five to ten minutes so you don't have to worry about the time. If the timer is on your phone, put it on silent or in airplane mode before beginning the practice to avoid being distracted during the practice.

You can read the upcoming instructions aloud and record them for yourself the first time, then play the recording back to yourself when you do the body scan in the future. Alternatively, a friend or family member can guide you through this practice.

During this, and all mindfulness practices, there is nothing to accomplish or change, no right or wrong way to do it. While you are scanning your body, if you get distracted, your mind wanders, or you notice a physical sensation, don't worry. That is what minds do—they get distracted, wander, and notice things. Because you are human, it is normal and natural to judge during the practice. For example, you might notice a judgment popping up toward yourself and how you are failing to be mindful because your mind keeps wandering to other thoughts about your day. The practice is also about noticing judgments as they arise and returning to the practice. More importantly, don't be hard on yourself. Do what you need to do to feel comfortable (like scratching that pesky itch or sneezing!) and gently remind yourself to return to the practice where you left off. Just bringing awareness to the fact that you got distracted is already practicing mindfulness!

connecting to your body: the body scan mindfulness practice

getting comfortable

If possible, lie on your back in a comfortable position, with your legs straight and your arms at your sides. You can also sit in a chair, with your feet on the floor and your hands in your lap or by your sides. Close your eyes if you feel comfortable doing so. Notice what your body is in contact with. You might do some grounding based on what you have already learned: notice what your feet are touching, what your back is resting on— perhaps a couch, a bed, carpet, or the back of a chair.

beginning the practice

Begin by noticing your body and what it is in contact with. By tuning into your body in this way, you are connecting your mind, thoughts, and feelings. Tuning in can remind you that you are physically present and can feel something, such as physical sensations that are here. Let whatever came before be part of your past and whatever will come be part of your future. Be in the now!

your breath

Next, notice your breathing—as you inhale, feel your lungs and ribs expand and your belly rise, then feel them fall as you release and exhale. Allow your breath to come naturally rather than trying to control it, trusting that after all these days, weeks, months, and years of breathing, your body knows what to do. It may help to imagine you are in a rowboat and visualize your breath as your anchor as you go through this practice. While the waves are rocking the boat to and fro, as you inhale, you pick up an anchor and dangle it off the side of the boat. As you exhale, you let the anchor drop to the ocean floor, where it settles in the stillness below. Your breath can be an anchor to the present moment and provide a sense of calm deep beneath the surface.

Note: *Breath is just one of the grounding focal points you can turn to in any practice. If it is too difficult right now to tune into your breath, notice your feet, toes, hands, or fingers.*

body scan practice

Now focus on the toes of your right foot. Without moving them, notice each toe, one at a time, and the spaces between them. Slowly move your awareness to the bottom of your foot, moving down from the ball of the foot to the arch and to the heel. Notice any sensations. If you don't feel anything, just notice what that feels like. After a few moments, bring your attention to the top of your right foot and ankle. Continue up your leg, noticing how your calf and shin feel, your knee, and your upper thigh. Zoom out and draw your attention to your entire right foot and leg, noticing how it feels and what contact it has with whatever surface you are on. Move from your right hip across to the left hip. Travel all the way down to the toes of your left foot, and repeat what you just did on the right side. Once you have completed scanning your left foot and leg, focus your awareness on both feet and legs. Take a few moments to feel gratitude for all that your feet and legs do for you daily.

Bring awareness to your stomach, ribs, lungs, and chest, notice the rising and falling as you breathe in and out. Move to your chest area and notice whether you can feel your heart beating. If you can't feel it, you can place one or both hands on your heart area—your *heart space*. Perhaps take a moment to feel a sense of appreciation for all the work your heart does to pump blood throughout your body every single moment.

From there, draw your awareness down to the tips of your fingers of your right hand, feeling each finger, one at a time, and the spaces between them. Start from your pinky and travel over to the thumb. Scan your fleshy palm, then the back of your hand. Slowly move up to your wrist, forearm, elbow, biceps, triceps, and shoulder. Move across the collarbone to the left shoulder. Draw your attention down to the tips of your fingers of your left hand, and repeat what you did on the right side. Once you have completed scanning your left hand and arm, focus your awareness on both hands and arms, moving all the way up to the shoulders.

Now move your attention from your shoulders down to your lower back. Slowly travel up your back, noticing your spine and all the muscles supporting it. Breathe into any tension you may be holding in your back as you move up to your shoulders and to the back of your neck. Bring in fresh, clean, cool air as you inhale. Let any tension or tightness gently release as you exhale.

Travel up the back of your head and move to the front of your face. Notice your forehead, eyebrows, eyelashes, eyes, cheeks, nose, nostrils, mouth, lips, teeth, tongue, jaw, chin, ears, and throat. Notice your entire face in your awareness. If you are holding a facial expression, release it. There is no need to hold any expression right now; let all tension melt away.

Take a moment to notice your entire body. Let any sensations come to you, just taking inventory of what they are—tingling, coolness, warmth, heaviness, something else—and accept whatever sensation is present as just that: a sensation that will arise and then eventually go away, like a wave ebbing and flowing. Scan your body from your toes to the top of your head, your head to your toes. Zoom out and bring your awareness to your entire body. Take several slow breaths in and out, noticing how you feel at this moment. Gently start wiggling your toes and fingers, inviting some movement back into your body. When you're ready, if your eyes are closed, slowly start to open them, gradually letting the light back in.

mindful takeaway in the moment   The body scan mindfulness practice is a way to arrive in your body just as it is this very moment without changing anything. It is a great tool to help ground you and tune into what is going on in your body instead of engaging in self-harming behaviors.

debriefing the body scan mindfulness practice: reflect on your experience

How does your body feel right now?

_____

_____

How has your body changed merely by your paying attention to and noticing it?

_____

_____

What was it like for you to notice how your body feels without doing anything else?

_____

_____

What different physical sensations did you notice in your body during the practice?

_____

_____

What emotions came up for you while doing this practice?

_____

_____

What thoughts came up for you during the practice?

_____

_____

Did you get distracted at all? If so, what were you distracted by?

_____

_____

If you were able to return to the body scan after a distraction, how did you do that?

_____

_____

14 bringing mindfulness into everything you do

for you to know

Amit Ray, an author and spiritual master known for his teachings on meditation, yoga, peace, and compassion, said, "Life is a dance. Mindfulness is witnessing that dance." Instead of just going through the motions, and rushing through your day, inviting mindfulness into every aspect of your life can help you be present to all that you do for yourself and with or for others. Being more present can enhance all your experiences, making them richer and more memorable, and can help you respond rather than react in all kinds of situations so you can write your story in a positive and nourishing way.

mindful or mindless—on autopilot?

Do you ever enter a room and not remember exactly what you saw on the way there, or even what path you took? People are often on autopilot and not truly aware of what they are doing or what is around them. In this autopilot state, you are mindless, not mindful, and you miss out on a lot.

Taylor was late to soccer practice and frantically texting her friend while running across the school campus. When she arrived at the field, her friend was laughing hysterically. She asked if Taylor had seen the poster of the llama on the wall by the locker room on her way out to the field. Taylor had no clue what her friend was talking about. She had been in such a rush that she hadn't even looked around. It was amazing that she hadn't bumped into a pole on her way to the field!

Being mindful is virtually the opposite of Taylor's experience. She was on autopilot, being mindless. Mindfulness allows you to experience something you may have done dozens or even hundreds of times as though you were seeing it for the first time. Think about a puppy going for a walk … he goes on the same walk, passing the same flowers, bushes, trees, and signs every single day, but each time, he eagerly wags his tail and treats it like an incredible new adventure. Wouldn't it be nice to see things that way daily?

mindful walking and photography practice

Mindful walking is one example of a way you can bring mindfulness to anything you do. The next time you are feeling the urge to harm yourself in some way and notice the triggers rising, try this practice, provided it is safe to take a walk.

Choose a path about ten to twenty feet long—this could be your front or backyard, your bedroom, somewhere where you live, school, or a nearby park. Your path doesn't have to be long because your goal is not to go anywhere. Take a camera or smartphone with you. If you are using a smartphone, it is advisable to put it in airplane mode to avoid other distractions; during the activity, the sole purpose of the phone is to take pictures while you walk.

For five to ten minutes, walk back and forth slowly on your chosen path. You can move your arms in whatever way is comfortable to you and hold your camera or phone however feels most comfortable and easiest to access. You don't need to focus on your breathing for this activity; just breathe normally and effortlessly.

As you continue walking, look around—really look around—and begin to pay attention to what you see. With your camera or phone handy, start noticing what you see—what draws your attention. Take pictures of anything that appears unusual or that your eyes focus on for whatever reason. It may be a red sign, a hummingbird or butterfly, a person jogging, a yellow flower in a field of pink flowers—whatever you notice or whatever seems out of the ordinary. Take pictures of anything you notice.

Your mind will wander while you walk; that is completely normal. When you get distracted, give yourself permission to stop walking. Take a second to focus on what it is that distracted you (whether it is a thought, a feeling, a sound, or an image), and then continue walking. What matters is being aware that you got distracted; noticing what distracted you, but not judging it as good or bad, right or wrong; and returning to what you were doing.

You can practice this while walking other places during your day, whether you use your phone or a camera to take pictures or just focus on observing your surroundings and noticing things you may not have otherwise noticed.

To learn about bringing mindfulness to routine activities (for example, washing your hands, brushing your teeth, making your bed), go to *Mindfulness in the Mundane* in the online resources section at http://www.newharbinger.com/43676.

mindful takeaway in the moment   You can bring mindfulness to everything you do from the minute you wake up to the time you go to bed. Bring fresh eyes to things you have done even a thousand times. When you are doing everyday routine activities, consider bringing mindful awareness to them.

mindful walking and photography debriefing

People are often used to walking at a certain pace and may feel anxious, uncomfortable, or bored walking in a slow, deliberate manner. If these or similar feelings came up for you, describe them here.

_____

_____

_____

_____

What other feelings (if any) came up for you during the walk?

_____

_____

_____

If you got distracted, what distracted you?

_____

_____

_____

What thoughts came up for you during the walk?

_____

_____

_____

What else did you notice on your walk?

_____

_____

_____

_____

_____

Now take a moment to scroll through the pictures you took and observe what you captured.

What was the content of the pictures you took (for example, objects, people, ground, sky, pretty or weird-looking things)?

_____

_____

_____

_____

_____

What did you notice that caught your attention?

_____

_____

_____

_____

_____

It can be interesting to notice what catches your attention from moment to moment—that is mindfulness.

taking a mindful pause to STOP before you self-harm 15

for you to know

It can be difficult to take a pause and stop before you engage in self-harm. When you are angry, sad, frustrated, or irritated, or having other such feelings, it is difficult to remember that this feeling state will pass, but it will. Like a wave, pain is impermanent; it comes and goes, rises and falls. Pain passes, and the more you can let it pass or decide whether or how you want to respond, the better you will be able to cope.

mindful pause

A *mindful pause* is a useful way to take space or time—even a few seconds to cool off. A mindful pause can:

help you stop yourself from engaging in self-harming behaviors;

help you stop yourself from saying something to yourself that is harming;

help you reduce impulsivity and reactivity (you'll respond instead of reacting to yourself or others);

allow you to process your thoughts and feelings before taking action;

defuse the urge or desire to self-harm;

decrease self-harming behaviors;

choose what, if anything, to do next.

take a mindful pause and defuse the urge to self-harm

When you feel the urge to self-harm, take a mindful pause and do one or more of these:

- Take a walk, if it is safe to do so.

- Hold an ice cube until it melts.

- Count your breaths (breathing in one, breathing out one; breathing in two, breathing out two).

- Pay attention to your five senses and any of your grounding focal points.

- Scan your body from the tips of your toes to the top of your head and notice what is there along the way—something new, something familiar.

- Notice something in nature to take your mind off things.

- If you have a pet, spend some time with it.

- Listen to one of your favorite upbeat songs.

- Interact with a friend who nourishes and fills you up.

mindful takeaway in the moment   When you feel like self-harming, defuse the urge by taking a mindful pause before reacting or following through on your impulse. Doing so can create a space and allow for a thoughtful response rather than an impulsive reaction.

STOP before you harm yourself

After taking a mindful pause, if you still feel like you want to harm yourself, use STOP.

Stop right now: Stop and notice the harmful behavior you want to engage in before doing it.

Take a breath: Take a breath before engaging in the harmful behavior. Just sit with the impulse while you notice your breathing. Is your breathing normal for you, or is it shallow, tight, or restricted?

Note: *If your breath is shallow, tight, or restricted, take a break; engage in one of the activities just suggested and then return to STOP.*

Open and observe: Open and observe what you are thinking and feeling right now. Open to your heart and treat yourself like you would your closest friend or pet. Check in with your feelings. If you are experiencing sadness, anger, frustration, anxiety, or other difficult emotions, observe them. Notice why you're feeling that way right now.

Proceed: Consider what you have learned by stopping, taking a breath, opening, and observing. If you still feel like you want to harm yourself, please contact an organization on the resource list in the back of this book or speak with someone you feel comfortable and safe talking to about this.

16 mindful messaging

for you to know

The norm used to be for people to interact face-to-face, but now communicating through a computer or smartphone screen has become more common—and so have misunderstandings. Have you ever sent a text or posted something online you wish you hadn't? Have you ever had someone misinterpret or get offended by something you texted when you meant it in a completely different way? This happens routinely, but it can be simple to avoid. Being mindful of the messages you post and send can help prevent self-harm, social anxiety, comparison, and feelings of rejection, thus leading you down a less reactive, less impulsive path.

tips for mindful messaging

For many of your waking moments and hours, you are either posting, texting, or emailing. But how often are you messaging mindfully? *Mindful messaging* involves being thoughtful about what you write, post, and share in the online world.

Following these tips can help you avoid engaging in self-harming behaviors, thoughts, and feelings; and reduce awkward moments, misunderstandings, and posting regrets. They can apply to posts, texts, emails, and the like.

- Check in with how you are feeling in the moment. What emotions are you having? Are you angry, anxious, or upset? Check in to see if your body is providing cues that you are in the fight-flight-or-freeze response. Do you feel tense or shaky, or is your heart racing? If so, you may want to consider taking a pause before sending that message.

- Reread what you wrote before you tap Send or post it.

- Pause for a few seconds, reflect, and make sure this is a message you want to send.

- Before you spend too much time believing a thought about yourself or someone else, ask yourself these questions: Is it true? Is it kind? Is it something I want to say?

- Don't rush your response. The world will not come to an end if you don't get back to the person in a nanosecond or post that comment right away. Make sure it's something you want to share or send. Ask yourself, *Is this something I really need to respond to? And when?*

mindful takeaway in the moment   Before you post a message or hit Send, take a mindful pause. Read what you wrote and ask yourself, *Do I really want or need to say this … right now?* Pausing can save you a lot of grief and drama.

practice mindful messaging and posting

The next time you go to send a message or post something, take a mindful pause and complete this activity.

Stop where you are. Be present and tune into what is occurring. Write down where you are, what you are doing, and the circumstances leading you to send or post something.

_____

_____

_____

How are you are feeling physically and emotionally?

_____

_____

Take a couple of deep breaths, perhaps with your eyes closed. What is your intention or reason for sending or posting the message? What impact might the message have?

_____

_____

_____

Try to answer these questions as well: Is it true? Is it necessary? Is it kind?

_____

_____

Now you can decide whether you want to tap Send or post.

What did you decide to do, and what was the outcome?

_____

_____

_____

What was it like for you to go through this process of mindful messaging?

_____

_____

_____

Self-Harming Thoughts and Feelings:

Ease Your Mental and Emotional Pain

17 self-harming thoughts and feelings

for you to know

Writer and psychiatrist Howard Cutler said, "To diminish the suffering of pain, we need to make a crucial distinction between the pain of pain, and the pain we create by our thoughts about the pain. Fear, anger, guilt, loneliness, and helplessness are all mental and emotional responses that can intensify pain." Having an awareness of the thoughts and feelings that often *precede* your considering or engaging in self-harming behavior(s) can help teach you how to stop the thought or feeling from leading to the behavior.

self-harm—thoughts and feelings

A self-harming behavior doesn't occur out of nowhere; there is some thought(s) or feeling(s) that comes before the idea, desire, impulse, or interest to harm yourself arises. When you become more in tune with and mindful of your thoughts and feelings that often precede a harming behavior, you can *choose* to do something different, rather than engaging in the behavior. This awareness gives you:

the ability to respond instead of react;

the power to choose how you respond;

the decision to engage in a healthy instead of harmful behavior;

the choice to put your attention elsewhere or to take a mindful pause if needed to help you respond instead of react.

Self-harming thoughts are judgments and beliefs you have about yourself, people, places, objects, events, or situations that often precede the self-harming behavior or act. A self-harming thought might be *I am stupid, I am ugly,* or *I am worthless.* Self-harming feelings are those feelings—sad, upset, frustrated, angry, pissed, miserable, overwhelmed, anxious, worried, depressed, and the like—that impact your physical and emotional states. Any one of these self-deprecating and harmful thoughts or feelings often lead to someone engaging in a self-harming behavior to numb the pain these thoughts or feelings are causing.

Your feelings can often impact your thinking when you start to think harming yourself will help with changing your mood. It won't!

stand up to self-harming behaviors

You can stand up to your self-harming behaviors by taking a look at the thoughts and feelings that often come before "it."

What are some thoughts you have about yourself that tend to be judgmental, negative, and not very kind?

_____

_____

_____

It can be especially difficult to pay attention to painful emotions you would rather not have. What are some painful emotions that you have?

_____

_____

_____

It can be helpful to notice what happens in your body when an emotion comes up so you can identify what feelings precede self-harming behaviors. Where do you tend to feel your feelings in your body—your gut, throat, head, neck, elsewhere?

_____

_____

What are some events in your life that are causing you pain?

_____

_____

_____

Describe anything taking place in your life right now that you might not want to be present to or aware of, that might be impacting your self-harming thoughts and feelings.

_____

_____

_____

_____

mindful takeaway in the moment   Information and knowledge can be powerful. The more you know about your thoughts and feelings, and where they come from, the more control you have over the decisions you make and the actions you take.

surf the urge to self-harm: SOBER

Psychologist G. Alan Marlatt created an acronym to help with responding instead of reacting, and to help prevent thoughts and feelings from leading to behaviors. Take a minute and go through the process of SOBER.

Stop: Stop where you are. Be present and tune into what is taking place in this moment.

Observe: Observe how you are feeling physically and emotionally.

Breathe: Take a deep breath. Center your attention on your breathing. Notice where you bring air in on your next in-breath (through your nose or mouth) and where you release air out on your next out-breath (through your nose or mouth).

Expand: Expand your awareness. Consider what will happen if you keep thinking this thought or feeling this feeling. Consider what impact the self-harming behavior will have.

Respond: Make a decision and respond accordingly. Decide to do something other than a self-harm behavior. Use any of the resources and tools in this book to do something different.

SOBER in action

Any time you have self-harming thoughts or feelings or when you have the desire to engage in a self-harm behavior, use SOBER. Think, for a minute or two, of the impulses you have had to harm yourself, either in the past or present, and write down what comes to mind.

_____

_____

_____

_____

Now use SOBER:

Stop

Where are you?

_____

What is taking place right now?

_____

_____

Observe

How are you feeling physically? What physical sensations do you notice?

_____

_____

How are you feeling emotionally?

_____

_____

_____

Breathe

Take a deep breath. Center your attention on your breathing.

How do you feel now?

_____

_____

Expand

Expand your awareness.

What thoughts are present right now?

_____

_____

_____

What will happen if you keep thinking about this self-harming thought?

_____

_____

_____

What will happen if you keep feeling this self-harming feeling?

_____

_____

_____

What impact will the self-harming behavior have if you engage in it?

_____

_____

_____

Respond

Using any of the resources and tools in this book, make a decision and respond accordingly by doing something other than self-harm.

What action(s) will you take?

_____

_____

_____

Remember, you can use SOBER to:

    stop self-harming thoughts;

    stop self-harming feelings;

    stop self-harming behaviors;

    manage urges and cravings;

    cope with difficult triggers;

    handle high-risk situations;

    make thoughtful decisions.

awareness: where do you put your attention? 18

for you to know

William James, the first author to offer a psychology course in the United States, said, "The greatest weapon against stress is our ability to choose one thought over another." Managing stress is about *choice awareness*—where you choose to put your attention. You have the opportunity every minute of every day to make that choice. Do you attend to that which harms and drains you—the negative, the unpleasant, worries, stressors, to-do lists, pressures? Or do you attend to that which helps and nourishes you—the positive, the pleasant, what is working in your life, your basic needs that are being met (clothes, food, shelter, water)?

Make the active choice to direct your attention away from self-harming thoughts and feelings and instead toward useful thoughts and feelings.

spacious and directed awareness

You have learned that mindfulness involves becoming aware of and tuning into your senses—*sense awareness*—but you can expand this awareness. You can use *spacious* and *directed* awareness to decide where you want to put your attention. Think of the camera on your phone: you can zoom out and see the entirety of the landscape or setting—spacious awareness; or you can zoom in and focus in on something specific, a piece of the larger whole—directed awareness.

engage in spacious awareness: zoom out

Spacious awareness is paying attention to all you can notice, the entirety of what is around you in your environment. Imagine you are on a school campus. You can be aware of the entire landscape, all of the school. Think of yourself in nature, noticing the entire forest or beach in front of you. Or see yourself even in front of where you live, taking in the spaciousness of what surrounds you.

What is in your environment right now? Zoom out to see everything around you. What do you see? Write or list all you can see in front of you, around you, and behind you.

_____

_____

_____

_____

engage in directed awareness: zoom in

Once you are aware of your surroundings, you can make the choice of where you want to put your attention. Gain awareness, then choose where to attend. *Directed awareness* involves just that: choosing where to focus your attention—zooming in. For example, say you are at the beach and you want to practice noticing your senses. You start by focusing broadly on the entire shoreline, then you focus only on the sand right under your feet, and then you draw your attention more specifically to a tiny grain of sand glimmering in the sunlight. Direct your attention to one part of your surroundings and zoom in to one part of what you see.

Describe, write, or list all you can see.

_____

_____

_____

_____

mindful takeaway in the moment   You can begin by learning to have spacious awareness of your thoughts and feelings as they arise, just as you would with your physical environment and surroundings. Work on zooming in and out of situations to see things from different points of view. To put things into focus, consider taking a step away or a brief pause, and then refocus. Use these tools to see people, places, objects, and events more clearly and to direct your attention away from self-harming thoughts and feelings toward more nourishing and positive ones.

awareness of self-harm

Just as you can choose where you put your attention to what you see in your landscape and surroundings, the same is true of your thoughts and feelings. After you begin noticing what thoughts or judgments pop up, you can start to shift your attention to another thought or feeling. If you find that certain thoughts or feelings do not serve or support you or are making you more likely to harm yourself, turn your attention to something healthier and more positive. Choosing where you put your time, energy, and attention gives you a sense of agency, power, and control over your body, mind, attitudes, thoughts, and feelings. Once you are being intentional about paying attention, then you can make a conscious choice about whether you want to keep your attention where it is or move it to something else. You have the choice—you have agency, power, and control.

Think back to a time when you engaged in a self-harming behavior. This request is not intended to bring up old pains, but to help you look differently at what happened.

Look at all the aspects of this memory. Who was involved? What was involved? Where were you? When was it? Why did it lead to you wanting to harm yourself? What thoughts or feelings do you remember about this time? See the entire picture of that moment—zoom out.

Taking a step back and witnessing the moment can often be easier when you have some distance from it. If you are zoomed in and too tightly connected to one part of the moment, it helps to zoom out and notice all the pieces instead of just the one you are focused on.

In the memory you are reflecting on, can you see whether you were zoomed in, overly focused or connected to one or more pieces—the person, the event, the feeling—rather than focused on all the pieces?

You can choose to shift your attention. If you are zoomed out, try zooming in; if you are zoomed in, try zooming out.

quieting the judgmental mind 19

for you to know

The idea of the "monkey mind" swinging from branch to branch is commonly used in the world of mindfulness. Your brain is constantly working, creating new neural connections every moment; you have countless thoughts racing around in the jungle of your mind on a regular basis. This activity is about becoming aware of what is going on in that jungle of your mind and learning to identify which thoughts are helpful and true and which are harmful and false, or not based in reality. By doing so, you can then learn to give more attention to the helpful and true thoughts, as well as create more of them, and ideally reduce or eliminate self-harming ones.

food for thought: a thought is just a thought

Here is some food for thought about thoughts in general:

- A thought is just a thought.

- Not all thoughts are true.

- Just because you believe something doesn't mean you need to devote any time, attention, or energy to it.

- A judgment is a type of thought.

- A judgment that persists becomes a belief.

- Judgments can be harmful when they are negative or critical and can be misinterpreted as true. They can also lead to self-harming behaviors.

Before you spend too much time believing a negative or critical thought about yourself or someone else, ask yourself these questions: Is it true? Is it real? Is it factual?

traffic in your head: observing your thoughts

Close your eyes for a minute. Imagine yourself sitting on the curb of a busy street, watching the cars rush by in front of you. Picture those cars as representing your thoughts passing by; some cars are self-harming thoughts, and these are just a few among many other thoughts rushing by. Just observe all of them, noticing as they come and go. You may see the same, or similar, cars rush by a few times. You may notice some cars cruising by slowly and others racing by at a fast pace. Just witness them as an outside observer, paying attention to what thoughts appear and watching them fade and disappear in the distance.

If you get distracted, just notice that and then bring your awareness back to the street and the cars. If you get caught up in a specific thought and suddenly notice that you are now inside one of the moving cars, calmly and casually let yourself out once the car comes to a halt and walk back over to the curb. Sit down again and continue watching as an outside observer.

In the space below, draw a picture of the street and the cars representing your thoughts, self-harming or otherwise.

Describe the experience of observing your thoughts without trying to change them. What was it like to sit on the curb and observe your thoughts as they passed by?

_____

_____

_____

_____

_____

What kinds of thoughts came up?

_____

_____

_____

_____

_____

If you got distracted or carried away in one of your thoughts (riding in a car), what was that like? Describe the thoughts that distracted you? How were you able to get back to the curb and bring your attention back to observing your thoughts?

_____

_____

_____

_____

mindful takeaway in the moment   Before you believe something you think, especially if it is self-harming and critical, check in and ask yourself whether you are absolutely sure it is true, real, and factual. Remain curious. Remember that harmful judgments are often mistakenly adopted as truths about yourself and the world.

judgments: fact or fiction?

Taking a thought that is a judgment and treating it as a fact can be a recipe for disaster. A judgment is open to interpretation; it can be challenged, questioned, and disputed. A fact, on the other hand, has cold, hard evidence proving it is true. Learning to discriminate between the two and starting to question your judgments, especially those harmful untruths that cause you to criticize yourself or someone else and often lead to self-harming behaviors, can be extremely helpful. Here are some examples:

- I got a C on my test (*fact*). I am stupid and worthless (*judgment*). This judgment led to my feeling depressed and having the desire to isolate and pop some pills.

- I ate two doughnuts this morning (*fact*). I am fat and have no self-control (*judgment*). This judgment led to my starving myself all day, then bingeing on pizza and cereal late at night.

- Jason laughed at me when I missed the ball (*fact*). He must think I am a horrible athlete and shouldn't be starting in the game (*judgment*). This judgment made me feel insecure, angry, and embarrassed, and I had the urge to cut myself.

Often, such negative thinking associated with harmful judgments leads to painful and stressful feelings and triggers self-harming behaviors, as shown in the above examples. Whenever you get caught up in negative thinking, it can be helpful to ask yourself whether you are 100 percent certain, beyond a shadow of a doubt, that the thought is true, real, and factual.

20 the thinking trap: past-now-future

for you to know

"The secret of health for both mind and body is not to mourn for the past, worry about the future, or anticipate troubles, but to live in the present moment wisely and earnestly." This quote from Buddha captures the essence of mindfulness and the importance of living in the now. Thoughts are extremely powerful and are closely connected to your feelings and behaviors. Often, being stuck thinking about the past creates feelings of depression; think of the three Rs: rumination, regret, remorse. On the contrary, obsessing and worrying about the future and what might happen fuels worries. This anxiety can lead to trying to predict outcomes.

Past and future thinking are often linked to the desire or urge to self-harm. The more you can be mindful—in the now and working to enjoy each moment as it comes—the happier and more at peace you will be, reducing and even eliminating the urges or desires to self-harm.

where are your thoughts right now?

In the space below, take one or two minutes to write down every single thought that comes to your mind—or until you run out of lines. Set a timer for yourself if you can, perhaps on your phone or a kitchen timer if you have access to one nearby. Don't worry about writing complete sentences, having proper grammar, or censoring the thoughts you have. Just freewrite every little thing that pops into your head, one thought per line.

_____

_____

_____

_____

_____

_____

_____

_____

_____

_____

_____

_____

_____

_____

_____

Now go back through and categorize each thought. Write a *P* next to every thought that had something to do with the past. Write an *N* next to each one that involved the now, or the present moment. Write an *F* next to thoughts that dealt with the future.

How many of each did you have? Write the totals here:

Ps: _____

Ns: _____

Fs: _____

Were you mostly thinking about the past, present (now), or future?

_____

What was the quality of your thoughts? Were they mostly helpful, harmful, hopeful, hopeless, healthy, unhealthy…?

Ps: _____

Ns: _____

Fs: _____

Often, people cope with negative P and F thoughts by harming themselves in some way as an unhealthy form of distraction. Have any of these types of negative thoughts led you to self-harm? If so, explain.

_____

_____

_____

What are you missing out on in the now—the present moment—by reflecting on what has already happened in the past or thinking about what could happen in the future?

_____

_____

_____

mindful takeaway in the moment   Eckhart Tolle, spiritual teacher and author of *The Power of Now,* summed it up perfectly: "Unease, anxiety, tension, stress, worry—all forms of fear—are caused by too much future, and not enough presence. Guilt, regret, resentment, grievances, sadness, bitterness, and all forms of nonforgiveness are caused by too much past, and not enough presence." The more you can be in the present moment, the better you will feel and the more fully you will experience life in the now!

the stories you tell yourself

Have you ever heard or read the same event reported in the media by two different people or sources in drastically different ways? How stories are told and how news is shared are highly subjective and based on a variety of factors: the storyteller or reporter's mood, past experiences, values, mind-set, and many other things. Similarly, the stories you tell about yourself and about the world—your mental news feed—are influenced by your past, and they affect your current functioning and relationships. Watching your mental news feed can help you gain awareness of how the body and mind react to thoughts and feelings. You can then start to rewrite your personal narrative—and reframe how you think about and talk about yourself and your life—to make it more positive and healthier, and to encourage self-confidence, self-respect, and self-love, instead of self-harm.

rewriting your story: P, N, and F

P: Imagine you are a reporter writing a short article about a past challenge that you overcame. Keep it short and simple, starting with who, what, when, and where. Include your personal strengths and any other resources that helped you overcome this challenge and learn from it. Write in the third person as though you're reporting about a survivor or hero—someone you respect and admire.

_____

_____

_____

_____

_____

_____

_____

N: Next, put on your storyteller hat. In the space below, describe your life now. Write a short description of yourself, what your strengths are, what things matter to you, what inspires and drives you. You could also mention your current challenges or obstacles, and how you're working to overcome them.

_____

_____

_____

_____

_____

_____

_____

F: Finally, picture a loved one giving a toast at your seventieth birthday in front of all your family and friends. You've lived your ideal life, and it's been amazing! Write the toast they give in this ideal future, including all you have accomplished and what they are most proud of in terms of who you are as a human being.

_____

_____

_____

_____

_____

_____

_____

21 knowing your feelings and the information they provide

for you to know

All feelings, even painful ones, provide you with direct information about what you need and what actions you might take to get those needs met. You can make a choice to actively feel and move through a feeling, or you can let the feeling stop you in your tracks and lead to self-harm. It is often when you are hungry, angry (or having other feelings), lonely, or tired that your feelings might be intensified or worsened and in turn you want to self-harm to alleviate the feeling(s). Instead, use HALT to identify your feeling and what you actually need.

The next time you have a negative feeling, ask yourself these questions:

Am I **h**ungry?

Am I **a**ngry?

Am I **l**onely?

Am I **t**ired?

responding to what your feelings are telling you

If you are *hungry*, eat something as soon as you can.

If you are feeling *angry* (or having other feelings), just notice it. Remind yourself that the feeling will pass and you don't have to act on it.

If you are *lonely*, see if you can spend time with a pet, a friend, or someone who brings you happiness and supports you. If you feel like you don't have any of these to turn to right now, you could turn to a good book, movie, magazine, or music playlist that boosts your mood.

If you are *tired*, get some sleep, if possible. Even a mini space away from doing what you are doing at the time, such as taking a mindful pause, might help.

If you are still feeling hungry, angry, lonely, or tired, you can try any of the mindfulness practices in Section 2. You can also journal about your feelings in the back of this book.

After going through these steps, how do you feel now?

_____

_____

Do your feelings feel less or more intense?

_____

For more on halting your fears, go to the activity titled *Halting FEAR* at http://www. newharbinger.com/43676.

mindful takeaway in the moment   When you are feeling a lot of feelings, ask yourself whether you are hungry, angry (or having other feelings), lonely, or tired. If you are, eat, notice, connect, and sleep or rest as needed. Use any of the mindful practices you've learned to ground and anchor you.

HALT awareness calendar

As you go through your day, there may be times when you wait too long to eat or don't eat enough. You may have angry feelings that you ignore or bottle up, or at the other extreme, react to impulsively by blowing up. This calendar (which you can download at http://www.newharbinger.com/43676) can help you track your hunger, anger, loneliness, and tiredness. At the end of the day, mark each that apply.

HALT Awareness Calendar

	Monday	Tuesday	Wednesday	Thursday	Friday	Saturday	Sunday
Hungry							
Angry							
Lonely							
Tired							

You can use this information to notice patterns and make changes if you find you are often hungry, angry, lonely, or tired.

for you to know

In the poem "The Guest House," the poet Rumi uses the metaphor of guests coming and going from your "house" to illustrate that at any given moment, you are presented with opportunities to welcome new feelings, experiences, situations, thoughts, and people into your life. Sometimes, just like real people who visit your house, these "houseguests" can bring you down, introduce negative energy, or create unwelcome feelings when they stop by. You may feel irritable or impatient waiting for them to leave so life can go back to the way it was. The idea of shifting your perspective, being a curious observer, and being open is a key component of mindfulness and can help you reduce or eliminate self-harming behaviors, thoughts, and feelings. Being open means welcoming in and accepting whomever, or whatever, enters your metaphorical house, embracing change, and remembering that guests are just that—guests—who inevitably will not stay forever.

your guest house

How do you interpret this idea of "houseguests"? Your response could be the same or different from the description above. There is no right or wrong interpretation—only what it means to you and how it relates to your life.

_____

_____

_____

_____

What are some of the "guests" (experiences, people, thoughts, emotions) that have recently entered your house?

_____

_____

_____

In what ways have you have greeted and handled these guests?

_____

_____

Can you think of any guests you have not welcomed—guests that may have led you to self-harm in some way? Describe these guests and how you handled them.

_____

_____

_____

What could you have done instead?

_____

_____

The last part of Rumi's poem says: "Be grateful for whoever comes, because each has been sent as a guide from beyond." What does this mean to you?

_____

_____

_____

_____

How can you bring this approach into your life on a daily basis? Write your ideas here.

_____

_____

_____

Draw a picture of your "house" in the space below. Include people, feelings, thoughts, situations, or anything else that has caused you any type of unwelcome experience, perceived weaknesses, failures, self-harming behaviors you have done or are doing, or anything else that comes to mind.

mindful takeaway in the moment   Experiences, people, thoughts, emotions …
they are all temporary. All things come and go, just as all guests who enter your house
can and will leave. They can be welcomed, learned from, and then bade a fond (or not so
fond) farewell as they go.

put out the welcome mat

Fear often keeps people trapped inside their houses, shutting everything and everyone
out to protect themselves from surprise or unwelcome guests. The more you can open
the door and welcome the unknown and uncomfortable, the more you will grow and
change, and the less trapped you will feel in your house and in your current situation.
In turn, this can shift and change your fear.

Remember, feelings can be seen as a gift of information; all guests entering your house
can be treated this way as well. Be open and curious, inviting them in and figuring out
what you can learn from them. Listen to them, and observe what happens next.

for you to know

Henry David Thoreau, a famous American poet and philosopher, shed light on the power that thoughts have over how people perceive and experience everything in their lives: "It's not what you look at that matters. It's what you see."

What you think can affect how you perceive others, the world around you, and yourself. Your thoughts are extremely powerful, and they can affect your relationships, your physical and emotional health, and your entire way of being! Those who self-harm tend to experience distorted (often negative) perceptions of themselves and the world around them at particularly high rates.

When you are thoughtful and intentional about where you direct your focus and attention and choose to see the good, the strengths, and the potential, not only in others but also in yourself, those things will become more present and show up more in your life.

you are what you perceive

Depending on a host of variables—your feelings, personality, interests, mood on a certain day, attention, and even how hungry you are or how much sleep you got the night before—you can be in the same exact place at the same exact moment and notice completely different things, having entirely different experiences from one time to another. For example, imagine that two friends are on a hike together when it suddenly starts raining. The first friend looks down, noticing the muddy ground, and starts complaining that he is getting soaked and that his shoes will be caked in mud. The other friend looks up and squeals with delight, noticing a bright rainbow arcing across the sky. They are having two completely different perceptions of the same event—simply because their focus is not the same. Which person would you like to be in this situation?

music: the soundtrack of your life

Music can affect your mood, thoughts, and energy level, and even trigger memories. It impacts how you think and feel about yourself, how you treat yourself, and your situation. Think of a song that reminds you of someone you love, or one that brings up a happy memory from your childhood. Is there a song you listen to when you are feeling lonely or discouraged because either the melody or the lyrics themselves make you feel comforted or inspired? Or is there a song you have sent or would send to a friend or family member who was having a bad day and needed a pick-me-up?

Think of a few song titles you associate with memories, feelings, experiences, or people in your own life. Write them here:

_____

_____

_____

_____

_____

your playlist

If you were to make a playlist of songs reflecting your current life, what songs would be on it? Would it consist of music that is negative, depressing, or angry? Alternatively, would it be positive, loving, or encouraging? Take a few minutes to think about some of your favorite types of music and, more specifically, songs that resonate with your experiences, feelings, values, relationships, or worldview … the good and the bad. Start writing your "playlist," including these songs.

_____

_____

_____

_____

_____

What is your most frequent or popular playlist like? Are there a lot of uplifting, encouraging songs? Critical, discouraging, or painful songs? Describe your initial impressions, even including specific songs or types of music that come to mind.

_____

_____

_____

_____

If you get stuck listening to a song on repeat that makes you think about how worthless, alone, or unloved you are, or how you aren't good enough, it's time to make a new playlist: to rewrite the story you tell yourself and the songs you listen to and sing about your life and yourself. Creating your playlist to be more positive and nourishing can be extremely beneficial and improve your quality of life.

mindful takeaway in the moment   While it is important to accept the range of your emotional experiences, both good and bad, the more you practice taking in the good and focusing on the positive around you and in yourself, the better you will feel and think. Create a playlist that includes "songs" or messages to yourself that speak to the full range of your emotional experiences, but are mainly inspiring, encouraging, positive, and supportive—a list you can listen to, to help you when you are triggered to self-harm.

seeing your strengths: make a new playlist

People often focus mainly on their negatives and weaknesses. Take a minute or two to write down your perceived weaknesses.

_____

_____

_____

_____

_____

_____

_____

_____

_____

_____

_____

Now, count them. How many did you come up with in a matter of minutes?

_____

How do you feel now after writing these down and seeing them on paper?

_____

_____

_____

How would your life change if you made an active effort to focus on your strengths, on what you are (and could be!) instead of what you're lacking? Take four to five minutes and think about which of the strengths below apply to you. It may help to reflect on what other people who know you have said, or might say, about you.

You are being given more time to come up with your strengths than you did to think about your perceived weaknesses because the brain is hardwired to focus on the negative for survival, so it takes less time. It requires more time, effort, and training to rewire the brain to see the positive, especially in ourselves!

Circle all that apply. Use the blank lines to write in any others you think of.

Confident	Patient	Strong
Loving	Enthusiastic	Gentle
Brave	Hardworking	Reliable
Intelligent	Funny	Thoughtful
Curious	Determined	Other: _____
Compassionate	Analytical	Other: _____
Assertive	Creative	Other: _____
Kind	Active	Other: _____

Pick one of these strengths that you feel *strongly applies* to you. Write it down, and describe a specific situation in which you recently demonstrated this strength.

_____

_____

_____

Pick another strength that is *important* to you. Write it below. What can you do to practice using or applying this strength in your daily life?

_____

_____

_____

How do you feel now after thinking and writing about your strengths?

_____

_____

Now it's time to write a full playlist for yourself of songs that encourage you to see your strengths—songs that make you feel motivated, happy, supported, loved, calm, or nourished, and capable of doing anything. You can pull from the songs you wrote down earlier: the ones that you associate with positive memories or that inspire you when you're feeling down. Add any others that may have messages for you related to your strengths; for example, the song "Be Brave" can relate to the strength "brave."

You can refer to this list and listen to these songs any time you need, especially when you're experiencing any of your self-harming triggers.

_____

_____

_____

_____

_____

_____

_____

Section 4

Take Control of Your Life:

Be a Survivor and Rise Strong

24 taking in the good: learn to resource yourself

for you to know

Rick Hanson, a well-known psychologist and writer, said, "Taking in the good is not about putting a happy shiny face on everything, nor is it about turning away from the hard things in life. It's about nourishing well-being, contentment, and peace inside that are refuges you can always come from and return to." This advice is so relevant to anyone with self-harming thoughts or feelings. Leading-edge research on neuroplasticity shows that the brain responds to how you use it, to learning, and to experience. By choosing to attend to positive or pleasurable experiences (instead of our automatic tendency to tilt toward the negative), you can create neural connections that tilt toward the positive.

HOT: keep your fire going

To keep a fire going, you need oxygen and kindling. Positive experiences in your life are like campfires that keep you feeling happy, content, peaceful, and with a general sense of well-being. You can have a beneficial experience, but there is extended value when you can keep it going by creating a lasting resource from that experience. You can use the acronym HOT to help turn any good experience into a lasting resource.

Try applying HOT to one of your favorite upbeat songs using the following three steps.

H: Have the beneficial experience. Notice a beneficial experience you are having or go and create one.

Step 1: Listen to one of your favorite upbeat songs.

O: Open to the beneficial experience. Be open to all you can during the experience. Stay with it while it is taking place. Let the experience become more intense. Open to it in your body. Connect how your body feels to your thoughts and feelings. Be present to your senses and to your thoughts and emotions during the experience.

Step 2: If a song has a good beat, move to it, jam to it. If you know the words, sing or hum to it. Close your eyes and take in the lyrics and music.

T: Take in the beneficial experience. Let the experience sink into you like water is absorbed into a sponge. Let the experience become part of you.

Step 3: Notice what the lyrics mean to you. Notice the instruments that accompany the lyrics. Let the enjoyment fill you up. Savor the sweetness. Give yourself permission to enjoy the moment.

Next, answer these questions:

What song did you listen to?

_____

How do you feel right now?

_____

What thoughts do you have right now?

_____

_____

_____

List five other song titles you would like to use the HOT acronym with. When you are feeling prickly, in a funk, or just not in the best mood, listen to one of these songs and engage in HOT.

_____

_____

_____

_____

_____

mindful takeaway in the moment   Do something you enjoy today. Turn your beneficial experience into a lasting resource by using HOT.

take in the good

Alone or with someone else, engage in what you consider a positive and healthy experience. Take time to practice HOT.

H: Have the beneficial experience. Notice a beneficial experience you are having or go and create one.

What did you do? What was the beneficial experience? Write about it here.

_____

_____

_____

_____

O: Open to the beneficial experience. Be open to all you can during the experience. Stay with it while it is taking place. Let the experience become more intense. Open to it in your body. Connect how your body feels to your thoughts and feelings. Be present to your senses and to your thoughts and emotions during the experience.

Write about what it was like to open to the beneficial experience. What did you do to open to the experience?

_____

_____

_____

_____

T: Take in the beneficial experience. Let the experience sink into you like water is absorbed into a sponge. Let the experience become part of you.

What did you do to take in the experience and let it sink into you?

_____

_____

_____

_____

25 gratitude and the 5 Gs

for you to know

"Gratitude is not a passive response to something we have been given. Gratitude arises from paying attention, from being awake in the presence of everything that lives within and without us." David Whyte, poet and author, described how gratitude is an attitude and being grateful is an experience. It becomes infused in your daily life the more you draw attention to it and practice the art of appreciation. Like the adage "You are what you eat," you are what you focus on. The more you pay attention to the positive and notice and appreciate the good, the better your world will appear and feel to you. Gratitude is an effective counter to self-harming behaviors, thoughts, and feelings. There is an abundance of research showing that the simple act of writing down a few things you are grateful for each day improves your overall mood!

an attitude of gratitude: your basic needs

In any given moment, there is more right with you and the world around you than there is wrong. This is often hard to remember—or believe—especially when you are having a rough day or week. To protect you, your brain is wired to notice what is wrong, negative, or not working properly. It is critical to build your gratitude muscles to counteract this negative bias of your brain by paying attention to the good, to what you are grateful for. Consider the basic needs and fundamental resources you have that allow you to be okay in this moment. Mark the basic needs that you have met for you that you can bring an attitude of gratitude to:

_____ Can you see?

_____ Can you hear?

_____ Can you breathe clean air?

_____ Do you have a place to sleep at night?

_____ Did you eat something today?

mindful takeaway in the moment   There is more right with you than there is wrong in any given moment. When you practice an attitude of gratitude, you actively take the time to think about what you are grateful for, you can also express your gratitude—to yourself or others.

gratitude and the 5 Gs

Moving beyond noticing your basic needs, practice acknowledging and appreciating the things that you have, the things that are going well, and the people who support you.

What are five things you are grateful for in your life today?

_____

_____

_____

_____

_____

Who are five people you are grateful for in your life and why?

_____

_____

_____

_____

_____

What are five ways you can express your gratitude to yourself and/or others over the next week? *(Note: These could be specific and small. For example, write a friend a "thank you" card for being awesome, or reward yourself with a bubble bath for stopping before cutting yourself.)*

_____

_____

_____

_____

_____

What are five personal characteristics or qualities you are grateful for because they have helped you or allowed you to help someone else in a meaningful way?

_____

_____

_____

_____

_____

What was it like for you to write these five things down and spend some time focusing on them?

_____

_____

_____

How do you think your day, week, and month could change if you practice being in an attitude of gratitude and thinking of things you are grateful for on a regular basis?

_____

_____

_____

26 focus on your strengths

for you to know

Nearly twenty-six hundred years ago, Buddha said, "The mind is everything. What you think you become." Modern science now echoes this Buddhist founder's pearl of wisdom, with neuropsychologist Donald Hebb offering evidence that "neurons that fire together wire together." What do ancient Eastern religion and modern-day Western medicine both encourage people to do? Focus on the good; train your brain to build neural connections that are positive, healthy, and strength based. This includes how you think about yourself. You can work to build yourself up, not tear yourself down.

focus on your strengths

It's easy for people to focus on their weaknesses and what they do wrong. Because the human brain is hardwired to hone in on the negative, people need to try to retrain their minds to see the good in themselves, others, and the world around them. Being confident, believing in yourself, and liking yourself is not the same thing as being conceited. Focusing on your strengths and the things you do well helps build positive neural connections in your brain that can help you:

build a sense of self-worth;

build your self-esteem;

increase your confidence;

learn more about yourself and your identity.

improve your relationships;

enhance your mood;

you are awesome sauce

Your recipe for awesome sauce can include tons of incredible strengths, character qualities, skills, and talents. As you move through the world, you may recognize or develop even more of these, so your recipe will grow and become even richer over time! Look at the list that follows and circle the qualities that apply to you. Maybe there are things other people have said about you, or things you know to be true about yourself. You can also circle things that are important strengths to you, but that you don't necessarily feel describe you very much—they are still "works in progress" in your life. Feel free to write in other qualities not listed here that come to mind. To come up with more ideas to add here, you can refer back to the list of strengths you circled when you came up with your new playlist.

Funny	Trustworthy	Sensitive
Caring	Inspiring	Peaceful
Kind	Optimistic	Disciplined
Curious	Loyal	Insightful
Athletic	Understanding	Analytical
Spiritual	Open-minded	Other: _____
Flexible	Cooperative	Other: _____
Healthy	Creative	Other: _____
Intelligent	Studious	Other: _____
Determined	Silly	

tracking your awesome sauce activity

For the next week, record one activity (one thing you did) each day that was related to or demonstrated one (or more than one) of your "awesome sauce" strengths. Use the chart below (or download it at http://www.newharbinger.com/43676).

Awesome Sauce Tracker

Day	What you did	Awesome sauce strengths
Example	Made my friend laugh when she was upset	Thoughtful, kind, caring, funny
Monday		
Tuesday		
Wednesday		
Thursday		
Friday		
Saturday		
Sunday		

What was it like for you to complete this? Was it hard, easy, fun, frustrating, or something else?

_____

_____

_____

Do you notice any patterns? For example, was there one strength that showed up several times or many different strengths?

_____

_____

_____

What strengths are you most proud of from this week? Why?

_____

_____

_____

_____

Pick one of the positive attributes or strengths that you feel *strongly applies* to you and write it down. Describe a specific situation in which you recently demonstrated this strength.

_____

_____

_____

_____

Pick another positive attribute or strength that is *important* to you and write it down. What can you do to practice using or applying this strength in your daily life?

_____

_____

_____

_____

How do you feel now after thinking and writing about your strengths?

_____

_____

_____

mindful takeaway in the moment   Develop a positive inner voice that is louder than the negative one. Celebrate your strengths and wins (and those of others!). Be kind to yourself and others in your thoughts and actions.

your biggest fans

Do you know what people like and appreciate best about you? One way to find out is to ask the people closest to you. If this feels awkward, like you are fishing for compliments, you can tell them it is for a school project or a workbook activity you are completing.

Pick two to four people who you believe know you fairly well. These can be close friends, family members, teachers, tutors, mentors, coaches, or anyone you've seen and interacted with regularly. Ask them to write down your best qualities and biggest strengths on a piece of paper and give it to you to keep. Collect these from each person you selected; compile the list and write down all the qualities they listed in the space below. If one is repeated by several people, make tally marks next to it.

_____

_____

_____

_____

_____

_____

_____

_____

What was it like for you to ask people what they like/appreciate/admire about you? Maybe it was uncomfortable or made you anxious; that is totally normal!

_____

_____

What did you notice about their responses? Were there any patterns?

_____

_____

Write down anything you saw that matched what you circled for yourself or added in your recipe for awesome sauce.

_____

_____

Were there any you were surprised about? If so, what do you think about what they said?

_____

_____

Write down any that were hard for you to believe or that you were somewhat skeptical about.

_____

_____

What would it be like for you if you could try to start accepting and believing these things about yourself? How would your life change?

_____

_____

_____

growth and resilience 27

for you to know

Jane McGonigal, successful game designer and author of *SuperBetter*, knows all about suffering and trauma—and not only surviving it, but transforming it into something good for herself. When Jane was bedridden and suicidal after a concussion, she experienced excruciating pain and hopelessness; she overcame this by creating a video game. Here's what she had to say about not only surviving but also thriving after a devastating or painful experience: "Scientists have demonstrated that dramatic, positive changes can occur in our lives as a direct result of facing an extreme challenge—whether it's coping with a serious illness, daring to quit smoking, or dealing with depression. Researchers call this 'post-traumatic growth.'" She has since turned her video game into a resource for people suffering from all kinds of trauma. Her TED talk on post-traumatic growth (PTG) is inspiring and can relate to your own growth and resilience in overcoming self-harm (and even trauma).

post-traumatic growth

Positive psychology research coming out of Harvard University and other well-known institutions has shown that people who have gone through something awful have more intense strengths than those without similarly difficult experiences. Because past traumas are often at the root of self-harming behaviors, thoughts, and feelings, this is important to know! Anyone who goes through a trauma can experience PTG as a result. What fosters this kind of positive growth is discovering your underlying strengths, building meaningful connections with other people, and finding ways to give back.

Mental health professionals evaluate whether someone has experienced PTG by looking at these five areas:

- Enhanced appreciation of life

- Improved quality of relationships with others

- Seeing new possibilities in life

- Greater number and intensity of personal strengths

- Spiritual change(s)

PTG in action

Think of someone who experienced a trauma, a loss, or something that rocked their world in a big way and has demonstrated PTG. This person may be someone you know personally or someone you've heard about in the news.

Write about the person and what happened.

_____

_____

_____

_____

_____

How did they react?

_____

_____

_____

_____

What have they described learning from it?

_____

_____

_____

_____

What specifically shows that they had PTG, considering the five areas listed above?

_____

_____

_____

_____

_____

_____

_____

_____

mindful takeaway in the moment   Challenging experiences, loss, and trauma can transform you in meaningful and positive ways. They can deepen your connections with others, enhance your appreciation for the little things in life, and motivate you to grow as a person.

how to experience PTG

In the section above, you reflected on another person's experience and how it impacted them. Now, try to apply this to yourself and a difficult experience you've gone through. In the space below, briefly write about a painful experience you've endured at some point in your life. Include who was involved, what happened, where and when it happened, and how it felt in the moment. This may be difficult to do. Give yourself permission to experience whatever feelings and sensations arise and know that you are okay in the moment. Remember that it is over—it happened in the past. Take a few deep breaths as you need.

_____

_____

_____

_____

_____

_____

_____

Consider what you learned from that experience about yourself and your strengths.

_____

_____

_____

_____

Consider what else you gained from that experience, for example, more sensitivity and empathy toward others who have gone through a similar experience, enhanced appreciation for your loved ones, or a change in your perception of the world around you.

_____

_____

_____

_____

_____

How can you use this experience to be of service or support others?

_____

_____

_____

_____

28 respecting yourself by setting boundaries

for you to know

If there isn't a fence around your backyard, deer will walk right in and eat your garden. Similarly, if you don't learn how to set limits, say no, and stand up for yourself and your needs, you may find yourself being pulled in a million directions and tapped out. No one else in your life is going to be the referee, blow the whistle, and say, "Enough is enough!" It has to be you. Learning how to care for yourself, say no to requests that are unreasonable, and stick up for what feels good and right for you are essential for your well-being and can keep self-harm at bay. Learning how to respect and honor yourself will ultimately help you be a happy, healthy, and balanced human who is less likely to engage in self-harm. It is healthy to create boundaries and respect your emotional and physical needs. You are important, and your time is valuable! The more you respect yourself, the more others will show you respect as well.

can you say no?

Think of a specific time when someone asked you for, or to do, something and you said no. Describe it here.

_____

_____

_____

_____

_____

What was it like for you to say no to someone? What emotions did it bring up (for example, guilt, anxiety, or fear)?

_____

_____

What were the possible negative consequences of your saying no?

_____

_____

_____

_____

What were the possible benefits of your saying no?

_____

_____

_____

_____

What was your biggest concern about saying no?

_____

_____

What was the actual outcome?

_____

_____

_____

Were you surprised by the outcome? How did you react and feel about it?

_____

_____

_____

mindful takeaway in the moment   Consider showing yourself respect by having the willingness to practice saying no and setting boundaries for yourself. Say no when (1) a request is unreasonable, (2) you don't have time, (3) you think it is a bad idea, or (4) it is causing you or others harm.

checking in with your body, breath, and mind

There are many situations in which you will be challenged to stand up for, prioritize, honor, and respect yourself and what is best for *you*. Here are a few examples:

- A friend begs you to help her study for a huge test, but you have *so* much on your plate this week that you do not have the time—unless you sacrifice your own sleep or homework. You don't want to be a bad friend …

- You overhear a girl at school spreading a nasty rumor about you to a group of people. You are hurt, angry, and embarrassed; your first instinct is to run in the bathroom and cut yourself …

- Your crush is trying to pressure you to stay out past your curfew at a party and pop some pills. Your gut tells you to go home, avoid getting in trouble for being out late, and stay sober. You don't want to disappoint your crush or look lame …

The next time you are confronted with such a situation and feeling conflicted about saying no, or are triggered to disrespect yourself by engaging in self-harm, practice the following mindful check-in:

Check in with your body. Notice where you are sitting or standing, what your body is in contact with, and what feelings are arising. Observe and honor the feelings, whatever they may be. Trust your body; trust your gut. It always knows what is best.

Check in with your breath. Notice the air going in and out; notice your chest rising and falling. Count for five inhales and five exhales.

Check in with your mind. What thoughts are coming up? Ask yourself, *What is the worst thing that would happen if you were to say no or not do the thing you feel the urge to do? Are you certain that would be the outcome?* Consider the potential benefits of saying no. Ask yourself what response would be respecting your own needs and yourself the most.

29 keeping your water bottle full with the self-care tracker

for you to know

New York Times best-selling author and speaker Mandy Hale offered a great reminder: "It's not selfish to love yourself, take care of yourself, and to make your happiness a priority. It's necessary." Often, people put everything and everyone in their lives first and neglect themselves. Doing things for yourself is not selfish; it is essential to stay alive, function, and be healthy. Neglecting yourself is a type of self-harm. Think of a seed in the ground—without the proper nutrients, water, and light, it wouldn't grow. When you take care of your body and your mind, giving them the proper "nutrients," you are making it possible to not only be healthy and grow properly but also to be happy, flourish, and have a more meaningful life—to be a survivor and thrive.

keep your water bottle full

Self-care is defined as giving attention to your physical and psychological well-being. A helpful way to think about the importance of self-care is to imagine you are a water bottle and the water inside is your "energy." You pour yourself out all the time into many "cups" representing everything and everyone requiring your time, your attention, your energy: friends, school, family—the list goes on and on. Your water bottle would constantly be empty if you didn't refill it regularly. When you engage in self-harming behaviors, thoughts, and feelings, it's like poking holes in your water bottle that cause the water to drain out. Think of self-care activities as the opposite: as ways to refill your bottle.

self-care activities to keep the water flowing

Below are some examples of self-care activities you can do to keep your water bottle full and take care of yourself:

- Get outside and move.

- Practice mindfulness and relaxation techniques.

- Spend time with an animal (walking your dog, for example).

- Do something for yourself that you often do as a kind gesture for someone else.

- Say something kind to yourself.

- Play one of your favorite positive songs (maybe even dance around or sing).

- Take a few deep breaths.

- Laugh.

- Take a nap.

- Exercise.

- Practice a grounding technique.

- Write in a journal.

- Write a thank-you note to yourself.

- Write down three to five things you're grateful for.

- Call someone who cares about you instead of just sending them a text.

- Create something, like art, to express yourself.

- Watch the sunrise or sunset.

- Look up at the stars at night.

- Cook a healthy meal, maybe with someone who fills you up.

- Go on a walk, maybe with someone who is supportive in your life.

- Take a short break, pause, or step away from someone or something that is stressful.

- Take a bath or shower.
- Smell something pleasant (a flower, essential oil, a spice, perfume or cologne)

Which of these do you already practice?

_____

_____

_____

Which of these would you like to try?

_____

_____

_____

_____

Is there anything else you do or want to try that isn't on the list? Write down any other ideas here.

_____

_____

_____

self-care tracker

To start filling up your water bottle on a regular basis, commit to doing one *quick-and-easy* activity every day that takes up to ten minutes. Then, commit to doing a *long-and-strong* activity once a week that takes at least one hour.

Use this self-care tracker to track these activities; you can also download it at http://www.newharbinger.com/43676. Record what activity you did in each category on each day. Use the extra-credit column for additional activities you may have done on a specific day. For example, on Tuesday, maybe you listened to your favorite song (quick and easy), did an hour-long yoga class (long and strong), and then went on a walk with your best friend (extra credit).

Self-Care Tracker

	Quick and easy	Long and strong	Extra credit
Example	Listened to my favorite song	1-hour yoga class	Walk with my best friend
Monday			
Tuesday			
Wednesday			
Thursday			
Friday			
Saturday			
Sunday			

At http://www.newharbinger.com/43676, you'll find *Creating Your Mantra*, an additional activity on self-care and rising strong.

mindful takeaway in the moment   You can't pour from an empty water bottle! To stay balanced and healthy, and to be able to help yourself as well as others, it's essential to take care of yourself. Self-care is not selfish; it is necessary. Try to do more self-care activities in your daily life that keep your water bottle full and reduce the self-harming behaviors, thoughts, and feelings that poke holes in your bottle.

your water bottle and cups

Draw a picture of your "water bottle" below and indicate your current "water" (energy) level. Is your bottle mostly empty? Mostly full?

Do you feel nourished or drained right now? Explain more below.

_____

_____

_____

_____

_____

Remember, you can engage in the activities above to add more water to your bottle.

Next, draw cups *below* your water bottle and label them with all the draining things you are pouring *out* of your water bottle—all the activities, people, places, or situations that you regularly put time and energy into that drain your water bottle. You might draw one cup and label it "school" and another one "family," for example. Or you can be more specific—for example, "My teacher always gives us tons of assignments and homework with short deadlines."

Now draw cups *above* the water bottle and label them with all the nourishing things you could be doing more of or spending more time on—whatever you could pour *into* your water bottle to help your water level rise. You might draw one cup and label it "painting" and another one "time with best friends," for example.

What do you think about bringing more activities into your daily life that will fill you up rather than drain you?

_____

_____

_____

_____

_____

What can you do to make sure that your water bottle stays full and that you don't pour out all of your water? List specific examples here.

_____

_____

_____

_____

_____

_____

for you to know

Pop star Demi Lovato shared, "I am a survivor in more ways than you know." You too have learned to be a survivor! Many people who engaged in self-harm have stopped hurting themselves. They have overcome and grown from their difficult and destructive experiences and gone on to live much healthier and happier lives. There are people who harm themselves who will say they are happy with hurting themselves. However, you now know this is quite the contrary; often people who engage in self-harm feel guilty, shameful, and even worthless, but not happy. Sometimes your mind might play tricks on you, and you might begin to believe that self-harm makes you happy or fixes your problems. Remember to take a rigorous, hard, and honest look at yourself—you know your own truth. When the urge to self-harm arises or you notice the thoughts and feelings that come before the self-harm behavior, ask yourself these questions:

Does self-harm make you happy?

Does self-harm fix your problem(s)?

Does self-harm cause you physical and/or mental scars?

Being a *survivor* of self-harm means:

having mindful awareness of your self-harming thoughts and feelings;

no longer engaging in your self-harming behaviors, thoughts, and feelings to the best of your ability;

learning and engaging in healthier ways to cope and manage your pain and suffering without self-harm—choosing to do something different (for example, self-care);

moving through, overcoming, and growing from the painful and harmful experiences—rising strong.

rising strong: you are a survivor!

You are …

A

Awareness: You have learned how to be mindful, spaciously and directedly aware. You can choose where to put your attention. You can respond instead of automatically react.

SURVIVOR

Strengths: You have many strengths to help you cope and manage painful situations. You can use these strengths to make different choices and take new paths.

Unique: Don't try to be anyone else. They are already themselves. You are you, with your gifts, flaws, talents, and imperfections. You are, like every human, perfectly imperfect.

Respect: You deserve self-respect and respect from others. Don't let others tear you down. Haters are going to hate. Hang with those who lift you up, not those who bring you down.

Values: Values are the qualities you consider important to you and a way to live your life. Use these to guide your actions and choices.

Intuition: Trust your gut. Sometimes people can get stuck in their heads. When in doubt, check in with how you feel physically—take a "gut check," and if it doesn't feel right, let this awareness guide your decision-making process and do something different.

Valuable: No one is going to value you as much as you do or can. It is so important to value all the parts of yourself and realize you do, in fact, have worth. Self-care is a great way to show yourself how valuable you are. Setting boundaries and saying no are also ways to respect yourself.

Openhearted: Your willingness to share your love and express warm feelings to others and to yourself is important to feel safe, secure, and connected.

Resilience: The ability to bounce back and recover even after adverse and difficult situations, traumas, or tragedies this is part of post-traumatic growth.

take control of your life

English philosopher Francis Bacon wrote, "Knowledge itself is power." One way to take control of your life is through knowledge. The more you know, the more able you are to make thoughtful decisions and choices about the actions you take. The following questions can help increase your knowledge and the power to combat self-harming thoughts and feelings before they lead to behaviors.

Write about your awareness of your senses, thoughts, and feelings.

_____

_____

_____

_____

_____

Write down five of your strengths here.

1. _____

2. _____

3. _____

4. _____

5. _____

What are some of your unique qualities?

_____

_____

_____

_____

What does it mean to you to be perfectly imperfect?

_____

_____

_____

What does respect mean to you?

_____

_____

_____

Who are the people in your life who respect you?

_____

_____

_____

What are some of the values that are important to you?

_____

_____

_____

Connect your mind and body to make decisions—use the information your body provides you physically to connect to your thoughts. Do you ever have a felt sense or a feeling in your gut, a hunch, or intuition about who people are (good, bad, trustworthy or not) or about events (what is going on or how something might turn out)? If so, explain.

_____

_____

_____

_____

When something doesn't feel right to you, where in your body do you feel it?

_____

_____

What self-care activities do you like to do?

_____

_____

_____

_____

_____

What does self-love mean to you?

_____

_____

_____

Who in your life is it safe to be openhearted toward?

_____

_____

What are some current things that require you to be resilient in order to get through the angst they bring up?

_____

_____

_____

_____

mindful takeaway in the moment   Being a survivor means that every day you try your best to put one foot in front of the other and work to do the next right thing. Being a survivor doesn't mean perfection; rather, it is about progress and a willingness to grow, change, and look at yourself with acceptance and honest, open eyes.

break up with self-harm

It's time, with kindness, compassion, and assertiveness, to write a break-up letter saying farewell to your relationship with your self-harming behaviors. Let go of the power you've given over to the behaviors, as well as the thoughts or feelings that have been self-harming.

You can use these points to help you write your break-up letter:

- Acknowledge the self-harming behaviors that were there for you when you didn't know how else to cope with pain, stress, and suffering.

- Recognize whatever thoughts or feelings that would arise right before you did these self-harming behaviors.

- Acknowledge what you have learned, what you need, what is important to you, and what does not serve you or help you grow.

- Express gratitude for what you have learned. Perhaps you learned to become stronger; perhaps you learned something about what you need in your life, or something you no longer want.

- Explain why these behaviors, thoughts, and feelings no longer serve you.

- Share what you plan to do now instead of hurting yourself.

Use a separate piece of paper to write your break-up letter.

Looking at what you wrote, what feelings, thoughts, or physical sensations came up for you?

_____

_____

_____

_____

How do you feel now that you have written this break-up letter?

_____

_____

_____

_____

congratulations on being a survivor!

Now that you have finished saying your final farewell to self-harm, fold, crumple, or tear up your letter. Throw it away and begin the process of letting go. It no longer serves you. You can be free from the feelings, thoughts, and relationship you have had with self-harm.

pledging to stop self-harm

Now that you have completed these activities and gone through this journey of learning, discovery, and change, we, the authors of this book, ask that you take a pledge to *stop* your self-harming behaviors and the relationship you have with self-harm *for good*. If you are willing, we ask that you sign and date on the appropriate lines below; you can also download a copy at http://www.newharbinger.com/43676.

If you do engage in self-harm and have signed this pledge, please do not beat yourself up; change takes time and courage. Your willingness to change and your agreeing to *stop* self-harm are the most important steps toward the goal of no longer self-harming.

I, _____, pledge to stop my self-harming behaviors to the best of my ability.

Signed by _____ Date: _____

resources

emergency contacts

If you are in danger:

- Call 911 or go to your local hospital emergency room.
- Crisis Text Line: Visit www.crisistextline.org, or text HOME to 741-741.
- National Hopeline Network: Call 1-800-784-2433.
- National Suicide Prevention Lifeline: Visit www://suicidepreventionlifeline.org or call 1-800-273-8255.
- National Safe Place: Visit www.nationalsafeplace.org or text 44357.
- List of international suicide hotlines: Visit www.suicide.org/international-suicide-hotlines.html

mental health resources

National Alliance on Mental Illness (NAMI): Visit www.nami.org or call 1-800-950-6264.

Society for Adolescent Health and Medicine (SAHM): Visit www.adolescenthealth.org.

Love Is Respect: Visit www.loveisrespect.org, text LOVEIS to 22522, or call 1-866-331-9474.

National Eating Disorders Association: Visit www.nationaleatingdisorders.org or call 1-800-931-2237.

Erica's Lighthouse: A Beacon of Hope for Adolescent Depression: Visit https://www.erikaslighthouse.org/blog/.

LGBTQ resources: Visit www.glaad.org/youth or www.gsanetwork.org.

LSEN (an organization that focuses on LGBTQ issues in education):
Visit www.glsen.org.

Teens Against Bullying: Visit www.pacerteensagainstbullying.org.

Stressed Teens (for many resources on mindfulness, teen tips and tools, and
social-emotional learning): Visit www.stressedteens.com/community-organizations.

authors' contact information

Gina Biegel / website: www.stressedteens.com / email: training@stressedteens.com

Stacie Cooper / website: www.awareandthriving.com / email: drstaciecoop@gmail.com

Use this page for extra room for responding to questions from the activities.

Use this page to jot down reminders, notes, thoughts, or feelings.

Use this page to draw whatever you want.

Gina M. Biegel, LMFT, is a San Francisco Bay Area-based psychotherapist, researcher, speaker, and author specializing mindfulness-based work with adolescents. She is founder of Stressed Teens, which has been offering mindfulness-based stress reduction for teens (MBSR-T) to adolescents, families, schools, professionals, and the community since 2004. She created MBSR-T to help teens in a large HMO's outpatient department of child and adolescent psychiatry, who were not receiving relief or amelioration of their physical and psychological symptoms with the use of a multitude of other evidence-based practices.

She is an expert and pioneer in bringing mindfulness-based approaches to youth. She is author of *Take in the Good*; *Be Mindful and Stress Less*; *The Stress Reduction Workbook for Teens*; and the *Be Mindful: A Card Deck for Teens*. She also has a mindfulness practice audio CD, *Mindfulness for Teens: Mindfulness Practices to Reduce Stress and Promote Well-Being* to complement the MBSR-T program. She provides worldwide intensive ten-week online trainings, and works with teens and families individually and in groups. Her work has been featured on *The Today Show* and *CNN*, and in *Psychology Today, Reuters, The New York Times*, and *Tricycle* to name a few. For more information, visit her website at www.stressedteens.com.

Stacie Cooper, PsyD, received her doctorate in clinical psychology from Pepperdine University in 2009. She has counseled teens and young adults privately and in a variety of inpatient and outpatient settings, as well as led groups and psychoeducational trainings on adolescent mental health issues. She is certified in MBSR-T, and has facilitated workshops in community centers and schools throughout Orange County, CA.

More ⏱ Instant Help Books for Teens

An Imprint of New Harbinger Publications

THE INSOMNIA WORKBOOK FOR TEENS

Skills to Help You Stop Stressing & Start Sleeping Better

978-1684031245 / US $17.95

THE PERFECTIONISM WORKBOOK FOR TEENS

Activities to Help You Reduce Anxiety & Get Things Done

978-1626254541 / US $16.95

THE STRESS REDUCTION WORKBOOK FOR TEENS, SECOND EDITION

Mindfulness Skills to Help You Deal with Stress

978-1684030187 / US $16.95

THE BODY IMAGE WORKBOOK FOR TEENS

Activities to Help Girls Develop a Healthy Body Image in an Image-Obsessed World

978-1626250185 / US $16.95

THE SELF-ESTEEM HABIT FOR TEENS

50 Simple Ways to Build Your Confidence Every Day

978-1626259195 / US $16.95

THE ANGER WORKBOOK FOR TEENS, SECOND EDITION

Activities to Help You Deal with Anger & Frustration

978-1684032457 / US $17.95

newharbingerpublications
1-800-748-6273 / newharbinger.com

(VISA, MC, AMEX / prices subject to change without notice)

Follow Us 📘 🐦 📷 📌

Don't miss out on new books in the subjects that interest you.
Sign up for our **Book Alerts** at **newharbinger.com/bookalerts**

Register your **new harbinger** titles for additional benefits!

When you register your **new harbinger** title—purchased in any format, from any source—you get access to benefits like the following:

- Downloadable accessories like printable worksheets and extra content
- Instructional videos and audio files
- Information about updates, corrections, and new editions

Not every title has accessories, but we're adding new material all the time.

Access free accessories in 3 easy steps:

1. Sign in at NewHarbinger.com (or **register** to create an account).

2. Click on **register a book**. Search for your title and click the **register** button when it appears.

3. Click on the **book cover or title** to go to its details page. Click on **accessories** to view and access files.

That's all there is to it!

If you need help, visit:

NewHarbinger.com/accessories

new harbinger
CELEBRATING
40 YEARS